Remember When

Remember When

Robert Opie

B Bounty
Books

First published in Great Britain in 1999 by
Mitchell Beazley, an imprint of Octopus Publishing Group Ltd

This edition published 2005 by Bounty Books,
a division of Octopus Publishing Group Ltd
2–4 Heron Quays, London E14 4JP

An Hachette UK Company

Reprinted 2005, 2006 (three times), 2007 (twice), 2008 (twice),
2009

Copyright © Octopus Publishing Group Ltd 1999

Executive Editor **Alison Starling**

Executive Art Editor **Vivienne Brar**

Editor **Elizabeth Faber**

Designer **Dan Newman**

Production **Paul Hammond, Rachel Staveley**

Photography **Robert Opie**

Index **Hilary Bird**

ISBN : 978-0-753711-41-5

A CIP catalogue record for this book is available
from the British Library

Printed and bound in China

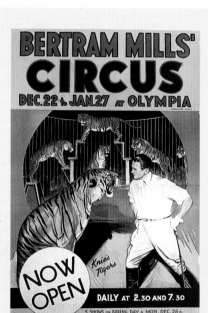
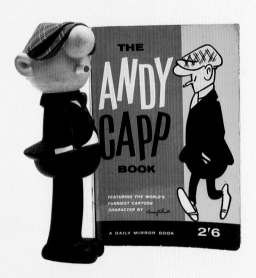

Contents

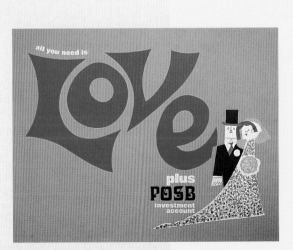

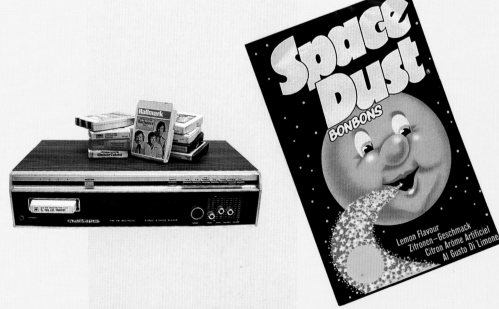

The Robert Opie Collection

Like so many ideas, the purpose behind the collection has changed and grown over the years. Initially, when – at the age of sixteen – I realised that the ever-changing branded packs of the self-service shopping era were, quite literally, being thrown away, I took it upon myself to save them. The bottles, tins, wrappers and packets that most people consider rubbish were evidence of a prolific and dynamic society – a system that delivered thousands of desirable items from every corner of the world virtually to our doorsteps. This was a feat that was perhaps more complex than sending man to the moon and yet was (and still is) taken totally for granted. But how did this all come about? I had to find out. I began my search for the origins of our consumer revolution by tracking down early packs and promotional material. Gradually, from all the assembled items, the story emerged. In a sense I had become a supermarket archaeologist or at least a consumer historian.

In 1975 part of my collection went on display at the Victoria & Albert Museum, London, at an exhibition called The Pack Age: A Century of Wrapping It Up. With much press and media coverage, the most exciting moments for me were watching the crowds of people throng around the objects, reminiscing with complete strangers about their memories. Even the museum attendants became animated and joined in.

By 1984 I had achieved my ambition by opening the Museum of Advertising and Packaging in Gloucester, Britain's first museum devoted to the story of our consumer society. It was now time to consolidate my thinking by writing some books – the most arduous of tasks, but they do concentrate the mind. *Rule Britannia* was published in 1985 followed by *The Art of the Label* (1987), *Sweet Memories* (1988) and *The Packaging Source Book* (1989).

I am sometimes asked why and how the Collection began. Having grown up in an environment where books lined every room and corridor, and thinking that every home had its own mini museum, it seemed quite natural to collect things. Indeed, this urge is instinctive in most of us, and many schoolchildren go through a phase of collecting stamps – I certainly did. But after a while there seemed little point in collecting stamps when I realised that everyone else was going to have a far better collection than me.

So I explored new ground by studying other areas of the postal service, such as aerogrammes, postal stationery, stamp booklets and greetings telegrams. This was my 'apprenticeship' in collecting. I was also fortunate in having the right parents, the folklorists Iona and Peter Opie.

When I began to assemble the story of our consumer society, it was like trying to complete a vast jigsaw puzzle of a million pieces. Thankfully it was not necessary to find every piece to see the whole picture. In 1985 an exhibition at the Trocadero in London's Piccadilly Circus, called That British Feeling, pointed the way to the next stage. This exhibition included much more than packaging, extending into my new interest in the artefacts of domestic life – toys, comics, magazines, postcards and so on. A touring exhibition, The Treasure and Pleasure of Childhood, went on display in Japan in 1993. My explorations into the consumer era culminated in the Museum of Memories at Wigan, which opened in 1999.

As is evident from the contents of this book, the Robert Opie Collection gives a sense of the different cultures and lifestyles experienced by our parents and grandparents.

◁ The components of my formative years. My first proper album for stamps that gave me an awareness of the wider world and a fascination with design. The early Lesney Matchbox toys carefully kept with their boxes, to which I added the date of purchase. The armoured car for which I saved 6d a week for what seemed an eternity, only to find that the gun did not actually fire as implied on the box (a lesson in life). The Munchies pack that I purchased in Inverness on 8th September 1963, the contents of which I was eating when I realised that the packaging should be saved. A family photo taken in 1956 – that's me at the top with my parents, brother and sister.

Understanding our past

'When you understand the past, the confusion of the present becomes clearer' – John Betjeman

Some people consider looking back at the past a waste of time and 'backward thinking'. Looking forward is the positivists' ideal. Companies, too, may take this stance, and while 'forward thinking' is associated with energy and enterprise, it is from the past that the lessons of hindsight can be learned.

For many the word history conjures up kings and queens, ancient Romans, wars and politicians, and catastrophic events such as the sinking of the Titanic. But history also consists of the small events that make up the daily lives of ordinary people. Here is the stuff of daily living, the very soil in which we are psychologically and socially rooted – here can be found the impulses of our society.

▷ Once upon a time parents read to their children; then radio began – *Children's Hour* from 1922, *Toytown* in 1928 and *Uncle Mac* in 1929. Television created a host of children's programmes, including *Blue Peter* from 1958. And now video stories – how technologically dependent will we become?

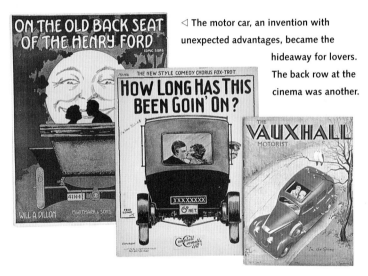

◁ The motor car, an invention with unexpected advantages, became the hideaway for lovers. The back row at the cinema was another.

If for no other reasons, our past is important because it relates to our origins, our cultural make-up and our basic understanding of who, why and how we have come to be. Indeed, the closer we come to the present day, the more important and relevant it is to our lives and those of our parents. Comparisons with the past are equally important. This is the only way we can discover trends in, for instance, the crime rate or the standard of living.

However, history is constantly under threat, not only because records may be thrown away (a reason for the existence of the Robert Opie Collection), but also because what survives and the way it survives may in itself be a distortion of historical facts. If museums preserve only the best examples, then we naturally assume that this was the normal standard. Equally, we may know the date when a product first appeared, but it may have taken ten or twenty years before it came into widespread use. Historical films may create

▷ The Ciné-'Kodak' home movie camera allowed ordinary people to record their daily lives in the early 1930s.

an idealised pastiche that is based more on folklore than fact and thus continue to distort the past. Moreover, it is human instinct to accept a story that 'sounds right' than to worry about a more complicated explanation. For instance, it became a popular myth that the children's singing game *Ring a Ring a Roses* was 'all about the Great Plague'. In fact, nothing can be further from the truth. This joke 'origin', started by Oxford dons in 1945, just 'sounded right', and is now accepted as historical fact. Newspapers constantly print stories that are not correct, either because they are hurriedly compiled, or because the full story has not emerged, or it is simply sensationalised – the headline itself can impose an overall instant misinterpretation. Our 'sound bite' society does not give us the time to explore the truth.

Our understanding of the past is never complete. We continue to discover new facts. As late as 1999 we learned that the aviator Amy Johnson was accidentally shot down by a British pilot in World War II, and the mountaineer George Mallory's body was found high up on Everest, suggesting the possibility that he may have conquered the summit in 1924.

Memories

As each year goes by another layer of events and images is stored away in our memory. The highlights will remain to the fore, others will sink into the recesses of our minds. Thus when trying to recall a particular subject, our memory will not always be totally accurate. Inevitably the greater emotion felt at the time the memory is registered, whether of joy or horror, the greater the impact and the sharper the memory. It has, for instance, become legendary to say that we can recall the moment when we heard of John Kennedy's assassination, and doubtless the same will be true of Princess Diana's tragic death.

△ The advertisement for Batger's crackers (c.1895) shows adults making merry at Christmas dinner; children have fun separately. By 1905 Father Christmas could be 'telephoned' (Hullo, or hello, was adopted as the official telephone response, bringing the term into widespread use). White Christmas, written by Irving Berlin and sung by Bing Crosby in 1942, sold over 30 million copies. The story of Rudolph the Red-Nosed Reindeer was written in 1939, and the song released ten years later.

◁▽ Childhood memories: helping with the gardening, at the seaside, playing at shopkeeping – and of course 'a visit to Toyland'.

Such memories are common to us all. At the other end of the scale are personal or family memories: happy events like marriages, the birth of a child and family holidays; or individual achievements like winning a race or learning to ride a bicycle. Other memories rely on an image sinking in day after day, year after year, which is stored away in our sub-conscious until one day an event unlocks the image – a familiar landmark is knocked down, a toy is lost or a brand disappears.

Each generation of children creates its memories from a different environment. A child growing up during World War I might remember, against the sad background of his father going off to war, the

joys of bowling an iron hoop or playing a boy scout's game. In the 1920s a child was likely to remember a favourite book like Mabel Lucie Attwell's *The Boo-Boos at the Seaside*, or *Felix the Cat* cartoons. In the 1970s a Texan chocolate bar or a Chopper bike might have been seen as the ultimate pleasures, while in the 1990s it would have been the Teletubbies or the game of Pogs.

Inevitably our minds are stuffed full of all kinds of information and sometimes memory can be triggered by a certain taste (as when, famously, Marcel Proust's memory of his childhood was released by the taste of a madeleine cake) or a particular smell. Who can ever forget the aroma of Timothy White's shops, dominated by carbolic soap and dog biscuits? And what more powerful evocation of a country childhood than the smell of strawberries and newly mown hay?

◁ Far cheaper than a painted portrait, the studio photograph became practicable in the 1840s with the introduction of the Daguerreotype camera. As with any new innovation, other photographic methods developed and gradually the cost of having the family picture taken was reduced. By the 1890s many people were taking their own pictures with cameras like George Eastman's Kodak.

For many it is the souvenirs acquired on holidays that most vividly bring back treasured memories, times of rare leisure, freedom from everyday worries and – in one of the best-loved phrases in the English language – 'time to stand and stare'. For those who lived through World War II, it was a time full of hardship and loss, but it was also more dramatic than anything that has occurred since and is indelibly marked on the collective memory of a whole generation. It only takes a packet of dried eggs or a ration book, and the whole ambience of the time is recalled – the air-raid sirens, the blackout, the songs sung by Vera Lynn.

Sounds play an especially vivid and evocative part in memory. For most it will be the popular music of our youth, the accompaniment to our formative years, when our senses are invaded by the new emotions of adolescence and we are forming our own tastes and identities. It is a curious fact that each new generation just happens to like the prevailing popular sound, rather than the one its parents liked.

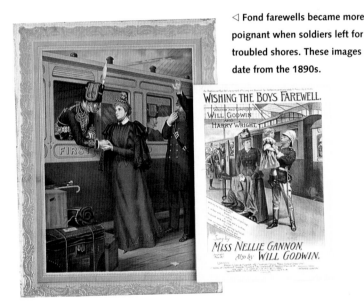

◁ Fond farewells became more poignant when soldiers left for troubled shores. These images date from the 1890s.

For those people who lived, say, in the 16th century there must have been far less to remember. In that time everyday life barely changed from one year to the next, from one decade to the next. Change was the change of the seasons. That was a time without memories of radio or television programmes, without recorded music and films, without magazines, comics or mass-produced toys, without fashionable clothes for the masses and without photographic mementoes of relatives and friends. What could they have hung on to except some whittled keepsake or handed-down folk story? Beyond the memories that are personal and familiar are the extensive collective memories that we can share with total strangers, because we have seen the same film or television programme, or have read the same book or magazine, or tasted the same chocolate bars. But as the multiplicity of products continues, the range of books and magazines extends, and the number of

▷ Rarely forgotten by those involved and often recalled with glee for years after (when the funny side could be seen), the family disaster became the key for many memories. In this scene from 1899, the hapless cyclist lands in the picnic lunch, while the dog runs away with the ham.

television channels multiplies, so the opportunity for specific collective memories diminishes, and all we may eventually remember will be a blur.

The widespread use of video cameras may capture moments to be replayed, but do we actually remember that event or simply the replay on the video? As television programmes are repeated, do we remember the first time we saw the programme or do we remember the repeats? It is the unexpected that often becomes the more vibrant memory. The Rod Hull and Emu attack on Michael Parkinson in 1976 or the extraordinary snooker final when Dennis Taylor beat Steve Davis on the final black, in 1985.

It is interesting to consider how, during the past hundred years or so, those living at a given time must have reacted to each new innovation as it happened. Things that we now take totally for granted were, in their own way, an amazing revelation – the aeroplane, the motor car or the telephone. How astonishing that it was possible to talk to someone hundreds of miles away, as amazing as the Internet is to us today. The first time that the mini skirt appeared in the sixties would have caused many raised eyebrows, as the language of the Sex Pistols on television must have done in the seventies, but look how quickly we adapt to such new situations and they become the norm.

By talking to our parents and grandparents about their lives and family memories, our own memories are, in a sense, 'extended' by their stories. This is why the images in this book will not only remind us of our own past but will also give us that visual reference for those memorable stories handed down.

▷ Sometimes the minor changes of life are the most irritating. In December 1983, the familiar metal lid of the Marmite jar was replaced with plastic. Cult followers went home and replaced the plastic lid with the old metal one or scooped out the Marmite into the old jars.

Our consumer society

In some ways life has not changed very much over the last 2,000 years. The fundamentals of living, our instinctive human needs, are essentially the same. What has changed are the aspirations we nurture and the standard of living we now enjoy. That change came about with the Industrial Revolution, when it became possible to provide increasingly higher quality mass-produced products for ordinary people – not just for the elite.

However, it is worth remembering that it was the privileged few who enabled the Industrial Revolution to gain momentum. As the moneyed classes bought luxuries they encouraged the market to expand and brought about the eventual reduction in price that made such items accessible to everyone. For instance, Heinz's pickled specialities were only available at London's exclusive Fortnum and Mason department store in the 1880s, and toilet paper was bought by the wealthy, while the lower classes used newspaper.

Before the arrival of steam power most work was done by man power or by horses – which were also the chief means of transport. Natural energy from wind and water was the only other power source – windmills were used to grind corn since the 12th century.

A major advance in human communication came during the 15th century, when moveable type made printing practicable,

△ **The tupperware and souvenirs of yesteryear. From left to right: Roman domestic pottery from London (1st century AD), including a drinking cup; a glass bottle and a bellarmine jug (c.1650); a commemorative bowl for William III's coronation, 1689; a mug celebrating peace at Amiens, 1802; an Admiral Nelson jug, 1805.**

though the cost of paper was still a restricting factor. William Caxton became Britain's first printer and publisher in 1479. By 1758 Samuel Johnson reported that advertisements had become so prolific that 'they are very negligently perused, and it is therefore necessary to gain attention by magnificence of promise and by eloquence, sometimes sublime and sometimes pathetick'.

By the 16th century European ships had started to sail all over the world, bringing back exotic goods like spices (and later cocoa, sugar, potatoes and tobacco). The accurate measurement of longitude was made possible in the 1690s by the invention of a

▽ **Once the economics of mass production were attained, daily newspapers and monthly journals became a reality. Left to right: Parliamentary Acts of 1641, including one to provide money for disbanding the armies and settling the peace of the two kingdoms of England and Scotland.** *A Perfect Diurnall of the Passages in Parliament* **1642;** *Oxford Gazette* **1665, published outside London while the plague was taking its toll; trials report from the Old Bailey 1679;** *The present state of Europe* **or the** *Historical and Political Monthly Mercury* **1692;** *The Observator* **1684;** *The Spectator* **1711;** *The London Journal* **1723;** *The Norwich Gazette* **1727; a tradesman's hand-bill for the grocer George Farr, who in 1753 sold tea, coffee, chocolate, sago, snuff and starch as well as rum and brandy 'at the lowest prices'. Other promotional items include one for Benjamin Piper's 'portable soap' (1782), Johnstone's Windsor Soap (1806) and a leaflet for the last lottery draw of 1826. The spectacles date from around 1650 when hinged side pieces held them in place for the first time.**

marine chronometer that enabled Captain Cook to make new discoveries and pioneer surveys of Australia and New Zealand on his second round-the-world voyage in 1772. Thus during the 18th century there was a growing feeling of enquiry and discovery. As the population in Britain grew (from 8 million in 1770 to 14 million in 1821), so did the proportion of people working in towns, creating a rapidly burgeoning urban economy. But manufacturing enterprises needed financial support, and this came from the rich and educated landowners.

The catalysts for the Industrial Revolution were inventions. Thomas Newcomen's steam engine of 1712 had been the first practical mechanical way of draining mines, and James Watt improved this machine's power and efficiency in 1769. It was this development that led to many of the rapid changes of the 19th century. Steam power transformed the speed and levels of production in the textile mills. (The textile industry had already been mechanised by John Kay's weaving 'flying shuttle' of 1733 and the 'spinning jenny', invented by James Hargreaves in 1766.)

At the same time building and engineering was revolutionised by the development of stronger and stronger types of iron. Abraham Darby succeeded in smelting iron with coal coke in 1709, although it was not until 1767 that iron rails were made along which the coal could be transported. The first iron bridge was built in 1781 over the River Severn. However, it was the faster puddling process of 1784 that made iron more practicable. In 1856 Henry Bessemer's patented converter allowed pig-iron to be turned into steel quickly and economically.

The key needed turning one more time to set the consumer society on its way. Distribution on a national scale was required. Raw materials needed to be moved and so did the finished products. Transport by road was slow, but a canal system could carry heavier weights, yet still be pulled by a horse. The first canal was begun in 1759, near Manchester, and by 1800 some 3,000 miles of canals had been developed. The keystone of distribution came when the railway system took off during the 1840s.

Now it was increasingly possible to distribute consumer artefacts quickly and widely and for newspapers to be circulated nationally. People could now more easily visit the seaside – the idea of bathing in the sea had become respectable ever since doctors encouraged it at the beginning of the 18th century. As more and more people had access to the same mass-produced objects, a nationwide collective experience began to be formed.

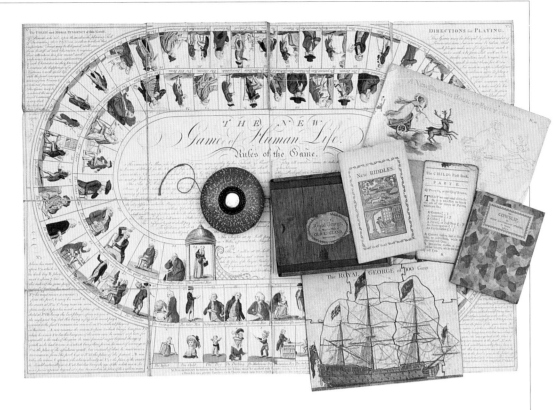

△ Playthings for adults and children: the game of Human Life (1790), a moral pastime that contrasted 'the happiness of a virtuous and well spent life with the consequences arising from vicious and immoral pursuits'. Known as a bandalore during the time of the craze (1789–90) but more recently called a yo-yo – the ancient Greeks also played with them. An early jigsaw puzzle depicting *The Royal George*, which sank in 1782 while being refitted. Some children's books: *New Riddles* (c.1765), *Child's First Book* (1785), *A New Drawing Book of Fancy Figures* (1803) and *The Cowslip* (1811).

▽ The race to the North Pole became an international sport in which Americans, Italians, Scandinavians and Britons all competed. Norwegian explorer Fridtjof Nansen's attempt took three years (1894–7), but it was the American Robert Peary who finally succeeded in 1909. Advertisements, children's books and games all captured the excitement for those keeping warm by their firesides.

The Victorians

When Queen Victoria came to the throne in 1837, the benefits of the Industrial Revolution were already being felt. The railway system was about to create an integrated economy that could transport goods quickly from the growing number of factories to the new conurbations. Souvenirs for the coronation of 1838 and Victoria's marriage to Prince Albert in 1840 included mugs, plates and jigsaws.

The Great Exhibition was held in Hyde Park, London, in 1851 to show off the 'art and industry of all nations'. The exhibition hall, nicknamed the 'crystal palace', was itself a masterpiece of engineering in iron and glass. (It was later moved to Sydenham, South London, where it remained until it burnt down in 1936.) There was great interest in the technological innovations that became the driving force of the consumer revolution. Over six million visitors flocked to see the thousands of exhibits – many came from overseas, and special railway excursions were organised from the provinces. For the first time public conveniences were installed, making a profit of £1,790 in just two weeks. This success inspired the idea of permanent public lavatories in London.

By the 1880s, for those who could afford them, there were many sewing and washing machines, mangles, carpet sweepers, knife sharpeners, gas cookers and lawn mowers (this last invented by Edwin Budding of Gloucestershire). Tobacco was smoked mainly in a pipe, but as machines arrived to make cigarettes they became cheaper – Wild Woodbine and Cinderella were launched in 1888. An increasing range of food products was arriving from different corners of the Empire to spice up the culinary delights found in *Beeton's Book of Household Management*. It was first published in 1861 and sold two million copies within ten years. In 1881 the first electric streetlights appeared.

In 1870 the Education Act made primary schooling available to all. Literacy was on the increase. The *Boy's Own Paper* (and *Annual*, see p. 25) came out in 1879, while the *Daily Mail*, launched in 1896, had reached a circulation of one million by the time the *Daily Express* arrived in 1900. The seaside visit became a part of Victorian leisure time. Blackpool erected its Tower in 1894. Gustave Eiffel had already given Paris its famous landmark in 1887, but Blackpool was first with lettered rock in 1876.

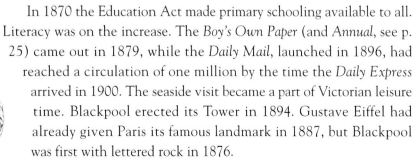

Travel and progress

The Stockton and Darlington Railway was inaugurated in 1825, when Stephenson's Locomotion No. 1 pulled 38 wagons. By the 1840s the age of steam was offering less expensive travel, in the form of passenger trains and steamships. In the following decades the rail network allowed people to live outside cities and travel there to work. Also, many now took the train to the coast for holidays and health, and to the cities for culture.

Before the advent of the railways, most goods were hauled on navigable rivers, canals – the building of which had reached its peak during the 1790s – and coastal waters. In 1829 the horse-drawn omnibus appeared, while trams drawn by horse arrived in the 1870s and electric trams followed in the 1890s. The world's first underground railway, using steam trains, opened in London in 1863. A deep-bore 'tube' underground railway serviced by electric trains came into operation in the capital in 1890.

△ The first railway timetable was published in 1839, and by 1880 it had become necessary to adopt a single time zone throughout Britain. This map shows the railway network as it was in 1843, when there were 40 companies operating 1341 miles of track; during the next two years of railway mania, an additional 5000 miles of track were laid.

△▷ The era of the velocipede, bicycle, tricycle, tandem bicycle and ordinary (later known as the penny farthing after its demise in the 1890s) was the 1870s. The advertisement dates from the mid-1880s, while the child's boneshaker was from around 1870. Its gutta-percha wheel rims were added later. In 1888 John Dunlop introduced the pneumatic bicycle tyre.

◁△ Candles were gradually replaced by oil lamps and gas lights during the 1880s. Domestic electric lighting arrived in 1896.

LONDON, BRIGHTON & SOUTH COAST RAILWAY.

NOTICE TO TRAVELLERS

COOK'S

INTERPRETER IN UNIFORM

MEET THE PRINCIPAL TRAINS STEAMERS AT THE CHIEF CITIES & PORTS OF EUROPE & THE EAST & ALL HOLDERS OF COOK'S TICKETS ARE ENTITLED TO THEIR SERVICES & ASSISTANCE

FREE OF CHARGE

Chief Office: LUDGATE CIRCUS, E
OFFICES AND AGENCIES IN EVERY PART OF THE WORL
PARIS, SWITZERLAND, SOUTH OF FRANCE, &c
Via NEWHAVEN and DIEPPE ROUTE.

◁△ Stage coaches had come into use around 1640; a 'stage' was the distance a team of horses could travel – about ten miles. By the time of this advertisement (about 1890), long-distance travel was being made by train. Telegraph poles – pictured here in 1892 – first appeared in 1843.

◁▽ Thomas Cook began to offer tourist excursions in 1841, and by 1874 was running an international network. With the increase in travel came the need for large hotels, and Cook set up a coupon system that enabled travellers to pay for rooms and meals in advance.

Mass production

The Industrial Revolution had made it possible to mass-produce all manner of goods, from brass bedsteads to biscuits, and the canals and railways could now bring them to the growing urban communities. To publicise new brands and products, promotional campaigns became commonplace, relying on hoardings and advertisements in the growing number of national magazines and newspapers.

Some brands were familiar commodities newly packaged – for example, cocoa was no longer just cocoa but Fry's pure cocoa, Cadbury's cocoa or Rowntree's cocoa – while others were new creations, such as Bovril meat extract (1886) or Bird's custard powder, an eggless substitute devised in the 1840s by Alfred Bird, whose wife was allergic to eggs. Fancy biscuits became popular in polite society during the 1840s, and among the leading makers were Carr's (1832), Huntley & Palmer's (1841), Jacobs (1851), Peek, Frean (1857), Macfarlane Lang (1886) and McVitie & Price (1889).

▽ Although most products sold by the grocer were still being delivered to him in bulk (tea, flour, sugar, rice, dried fruits and so on) a growing number of branded products were coming into the shops pre-packed in convenient amounts. This did away with much of the laborious task of weighing and wrapping goods for customers. The first boxed soap was Sunlight in 1884 (which offered £1000 to anyone who could find fault with it), and Lifebuoy soap came at a time (1894) when people started to understand the need for disinfectants.

△ One of the oldest chocolate manufacturers in Britain, J.S. Fry & Sons, had its origins in the 1750s. Fry's Cream Sticks were introduced in 1853, and renamed Fry's Chocolate Cream in 1866. This advertisement, from around 1880, shows Fry's large factory in Bristol, of which the firm was justifiably proud. Many companies promoted themselves in this way, for impressive factories reflected their commercial prestige.

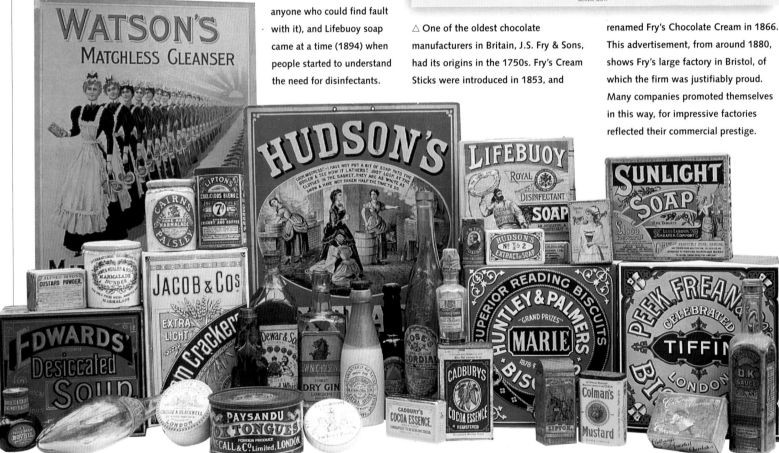

▽ The postman's knock became increasingly familiar with the introduction in May 1840 of the penny postal service, which immediately increased the number who could afford to send letters, Valentines and, from the 1850s, Christmas and birthday cards. The Post Office launched pre-stamped ½d postcards and a telegram service (1s for 20 words) in 1870, the Savings Bank in 1861 and Postal Orders in 1881.

△ In Victorian times the number of periodicals increased rapidly. News of the latest fashions spread more quickly now that illustrations were common. In 1848 W.H. Smith began to set up a chain of book stalls at railway stations, and by the 1890s had some 1200 branches. *Punch*, launched in 1841, was imitated in 1867 by *Judy*, which introduced the comic character of Ally Sloper (whose *Half Holiday* appeared in 1884). The first ½d comics were *Comic Cuts* and *Illustrated Chips*, both arriving in 1890 and proving immensely popular. By 1896 *Chips* – which was published by Alfred Harmsworth (later Lord Northcliffe), who launched the *Daily Mail* in that same year – was selling 600,000 copies a week.

Toys and books

The majority of toys had formerly been made at home or bought from travelling gypsies. But home-made dolls and hand-whittled tops, windmills, whistles and whirligigs were slowly being replaced by manufactured versions. Toys and games such as jigsaw puzzles and race games, once designed for the wealthy, became available to most families in mass-produced, colour-printed form.

Books for children were becoming widespread. *Struwwelpeter*, a collection of cautionary tales much parodied later (see p. 109), arrived from Germany in 1848. Lewis Carroll's classics *Alice's Adventures in Wonderland* (1865) and *Through the Looking-Glass* (1871) were illustrated by John Tenniel. In 1895 the artist Florence Upton created a 'golliwog' for her first book.

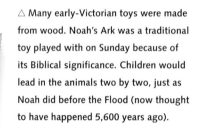

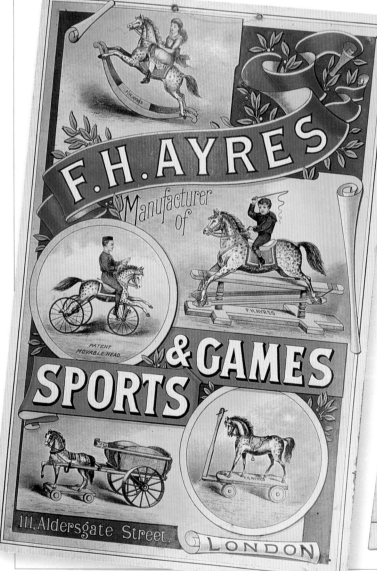

△ Many early-Victorian toys were made from wood. Noah's Ark was a traditional toy played with on Sunday because of its Biblical significance. Children would lead in the animals two by two, just as Noah did before the Flood (now thought to have happened 5,600 years ago).

▽ Building bricks, card games, race games and jigsaws were now available in attractive pictorial boxes. The game of Our Village dates from 1860; snakes and ladders came from India in the late 1890s. The two dolls wear clothes from the 1860s, when everything Scottish was in vogue thanks to Queen Victoria. The Ayres display card (left) dates from 1887.

△ Fortunate children could enjoy beautifully illustrated books such as Walter Crane's *Baby's Opera* (1877) and *Baby's Bouquet* (1878), Randolph Caldecott's *The Milkmaid* (1882) and Kate Greenaway's *Little Ann* (1883).

▽ Sticking scraps into an album was a popular pastime for young and old. The finely lithographed, die-cut and embossed images depicted a wide variety of scenes, including valour on the battlefield, for which the Victoria Cross was awarded.

Entertainment

Playing the piano, singing a song or reciting a poem were all popular family entertainments for children and adults. The musical box had become well established during the 1840s, and the organette had developed in the 1880s.

Moving optical illusions exercised a great fascination. Magic-lantern shows, which became popular in the second half of Queen Victoria's reign, were used for both education and entertainment; some used mechanical slides to simulate movement. The wonders of science had brought 'toys' for adults based on the persistence of vision, such as the Phenakistoscope, Zoëtrope and Praxinoscope.

◁ Sometimes known as the 'Wheel of Life', the Zoëtrope came on to the market in 1867. When the drum was spun each image in turn could be seen through the slots. As the drum revolved, the result was an apparently continuous movement.

◁ The 'new musical wonder' of 1880 was the Orguinette from America. Turning a handle drew a roll of perforated paper through the organ, producing music. The cheap paper rolls provided the latest in dance tunes.

▽ The film industry owes its birth to the combination of two ideas – the persistence of vision (here demonstrated by the 'flicker book'-type Filoscope of 1875) and the projected image of the magic lantern. Heralding today's television or cinema commercials, some food manufacturers supplied lantern slides for talks (especially for temperance meetings) that included an advertisement for products such as hot drinks, biscuits or meat extracts.

◁ Edison's Phonograph, patented in 1878, was the first speaking machine, first sold for office dictation. However, after 1895 the device was used to provide home entertainment.

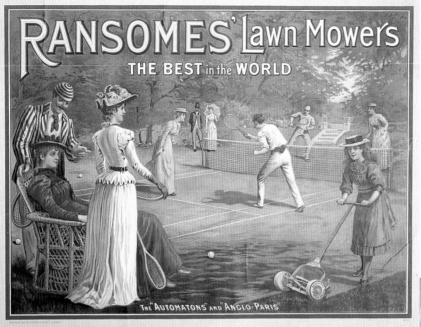

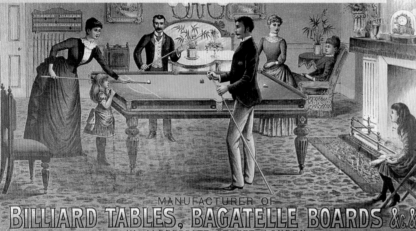

◁△ By the end of the century women were playing an active part in sports such as tennis, golf, croquet and billiards – but not football or cricket. W.G. Grace, England's most renowned batsman, played first-class cricket from 1865 to 1900, hitting 121 centuries. These advertisements date from around 1890.

▽ Victorian music sheets reflected the latest fashion and happenings: bloomers appeared in the 1840s and the crinoline from 1856; Captain Webb swam the Channel in 1875.

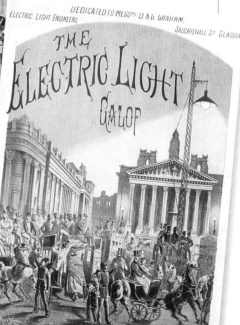

Royalty and war

After Prince Albert died of typhoid in 1861 at the age of 42, Queen Victoria went into a long period of mourning, dressing in black for most of the rest of her life. In 1871 she opened the Royal Albert Hall in London as a tribute to her late husband, who had proposed a centre for the arts and sciences. At this time there were many life-threatening diseases and royalty were not immune. The Prince of Wales almost died of typhoid in 1871, Princess Alice died from diphtheria in 1878 and in 1892 the Prince of Wales's eldest son died of pneumonia. The Queen had to be on constant guard against the many attempts on her life with pistols, and in 1850 she was given a black eye by a man wielding a stick.

Queen Victoria took great interest in affairs of state, and repeatedly came into conflict with her ministers such as Lord Palmerston and William Gladstone, although she both liked Benjamin Disraeli and approved of his policies.

◁ Song sheets, mugs and tins celebrated the weddings of Victoria's children – Princess Victoria to Prince Frederick of Prussia (1858), the Prince of Wales to Princess Alexandra (1869), Prince George to Princess Mary of Teck (1893) – Mary's parents are shown on the tin.

▷ The Jubilees of 1887 and 1897 were celebrated with pomp and circumstance, processions, bonfires and fireworks. On the earlier occasion, 30,000 children received commemorative mugs in Hyde Park.

By now it was possible to mass-produce decorative tins, mugs and knick-knacks. One song sheet of 1887 showed Gladstone with a host of Jubilee products, including Jubilee trousers.

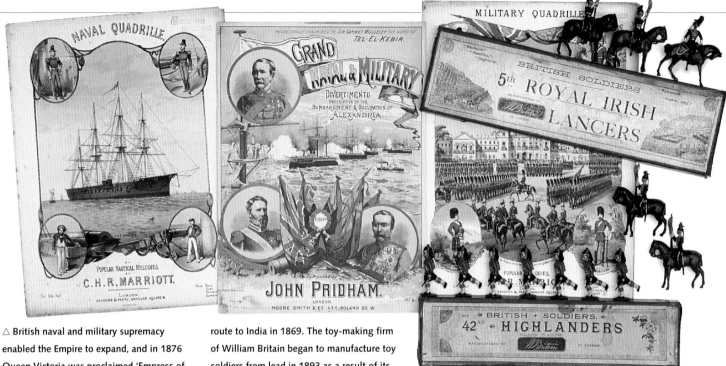

△ British naval and military supremacy enabled the Empire to expand, and in 1876 Queen Victoria was proclaimed 'Empress of India'. The Suez Canal had opened a quicker route to India in 1869. The toy-making firm of William Britain began to manufacture toy soldiers from lead in 1893 as a result of its invention of hollow casting.

△ Fighting flared up in 1881 between Britain and the Boers in South Africa, and more seriously in 1899, leading to historic sieges such as those of Ladysmith and Mafeking in 1900. When the war ended in 1902, many of its generals were fêted as heroes, with their images paraded on souvenirs, games and even scent sachets. Queen Victoria sent an unprecedented gift of chocolate to the troops to mark New Year 1900.

The Edwardians

With the dawn of a new century and a new monarch on the throne, Edwardians embraced the future. Motor transport was destined to replace the horse; a reliable car could be bought for £150. By 1905 there were some 9,000 motor cars on the roads, reaching speeds of up to 25 miles per hour. Accidents did happen and the London County Council set up an ambulance service that could be called from roadside telephones.

The Boy Scout movement was founded in 1907 by Robert Baden-Powell, the hero of Mafeking, who wanted to encourage a sense of duty and good citizenship in British boys. *The Scout* magazine was first published in 1908. Another movement was also gathering pace: the Suffragettes began to go to prison for their cause in 1905. Some women were now gaining reputable jobs as typists; this new role in the workplace was probably doing as just as much to enhance women's status.

Aviators were the new heroes. Louis Blériot flew into the history books with his Channel crossing of 1909, winning the £1,000 prize offered by the *Daily Mail*. The crossing made Britons realise how close they were to the Continent. In 1906 a new era of sea power was born with the battleship HMS *Dreadnought*; it made other warships obsolete.

Sending (and collecting) postcards took off during the Edwardian era, and in 1904 postmen delivered 613 million of them. An innovation from the Post Office was a stamp booklet containing 24 one penny stamps. New arrivals from the USA included the Gillette safety razor (1905), the first with disposable blades for the disposable age, and Shredded Wheat (1908), the invention of the aptly named Henry Perky. The American invasion continued with the opening of Britain's first Woolworth's store in 1909, with articles for sale at 6d or less. At the upper end of the market Selfridges, 'London's newest shopping centre', opened in Oxford Street that same year, and the day after Blériot landed his aircraft at Dover it was on display at the new store. London's electric trams had arrived in 1903 and the motor bus the following year; in 1905 motor cabs were seen on the streets and started to replace the familiar horse-drawn hansom cab.

Arthur Conan Doyle's greatest Sherlock Holmes novel, *The Hound of the Baskervilles*, was published in 1902. For children there was Kenneth Grahame's *The Wind in the Willows* (1908) with Ratty, Mole and Toad.

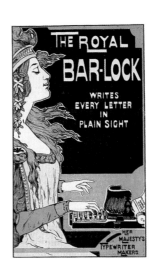

Events

Edward VII's Coronation in 1902 was the royal event of the era, but 1908 saw two other major events, both in London: the Franco-British Exhibition and the Olympic Games. This was the first time the Games were hosted by Britain, following the rebirth of the Olympic movement in 1896.

International sporting competitions were just beginning. The first rugby contest between two nations took place in Paris in 1906, when England beat France 35–8. In the same year, also in Paris, England also defeated France at football, winning by a whopping 15–0.

With the coming of the motor car and the aeroplane (see pp. 36–7) races were soon popular. The first Grand Prix was held in 1906, and in 1907 the opening of Brooklands Motor Course, at Weybridge, Surrey, was marked by a 24-hour race.

▽ The coronation of Edward VII was to have taken place on 26 June 1902, but the King fell ill with appendicitis, causing much anxiety. A slightly shorter ceremony was held at Westminster Abbey on 9 August.

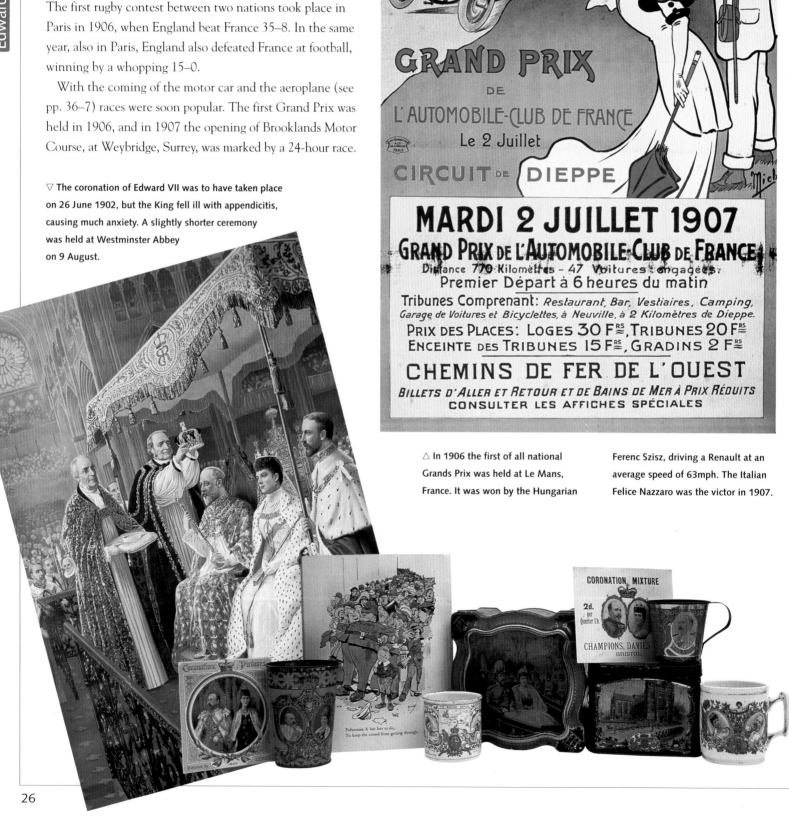

GRAND PRIX
DE
L'AUTOMOBILE-CLUB DE FRANCE
Le 2 Juillet

CIRCUIT DE DIEPPE

MARDI 2 JUILLET 1907
GRAND PRIX DE L'AUTOMOBILE-CLUB DE FRANCE
Distance 770 Kilomètres - 47 Voitures engagées.
Premier Départ à 6 heures du matin
Tribunes Comprenant: Restaurant, Bar, Vestiaires, Camping, Garage de Voitures et Bicyclettes, à Neuville, à 2 Kilomètres de Dieppe.
PRIX DES PLACES: LOGES 30 FRS, TRIBUNES 20 FRS
ENCEINTE DES TRIBUNES 15 FRS, GRADINS 2 FRS
CHEMINS DE FER DE L'OUEST
BILLETS D'ALLER ET RETOUR ET DE BAINS DE MER À PRIX RÉDUITS
CONSULTER LES AFFICHES SPÉCIALES

△ In 1906 the first of all national Grands Prix was held at Le Mans, France. It was won by the Hungarian Ferenc Szisz, driving a Renault at an average speed of 63mph. The Italian Felice Nazzaro was the victor in 1907.

△ Exhibitions were held throughout Britain but most notably at Olympia (built in 1886) and Earls Court (1887), which witnessed a stream of events. Around these sites attractions grew up such as the Big Wheel, erected at Earl's Court in 1895 to carry adventurous visitors 300 feet into the air.

△ The world's largest sporting arena was built for the Olympic Games of 1908. Much attention focused on the marathon, which was run from Windsor to the Olympic stadium at White City. The Italian Dorando Pietri was well in the lead but was disqualified for receiving a helping hand over the finishing line.

◁ London's huge Franco-British Exhibition took place on a 200-acre site containing 25 palaces and halls. The 'Flip-Flap' gave a view over the surrounding area from 150 feet up.

The domestic scene

Although the system of domestic service had grown up over the centuries and was well established in Britain, many home owners were beginning to feel the need to economize on their use of servants. To the aid of grand, and more modest, households came an assortment of innovations. These included better ovens, more effective cleaning and polishing agents (Cherry Blossom boot polish appeared in 1903 and Brasso in 1905) and better washing powders – Persil ('no rubbing or scrubbing') reached the market in 1909.

The vacuum cleaner was promoted as the replacement for duster, brush and broom, and even the servant. The original Daisy Vacuum Cleaner of 1904 took two to operate, but by the end of the decade the Baby Daisy was being used by the housewife alone, who could tell her maid: 'No, thank you, I can manage myself now.'

△ A constant stream of new food products appeared in the shops. By 1902 Scott's Porage Oats, Quaker Oats and the first breakfast cereal, Force, promoted by the character Sunny Jim, had arrived. Cerebos salt had been around since 1894 and the leading brand of tea, Mazawattee (1887), was joined by Typhoo Tea Tipps in 1905. Also available were Heinz Baked Beans, the relaunched HP Sauce, Ovaltine, Marmite and Colgate dental cream in a tube. Milk chocolate such as Fry's, launched in 1902 with its famous image of five boys, appealed to those with a sweet tooth.

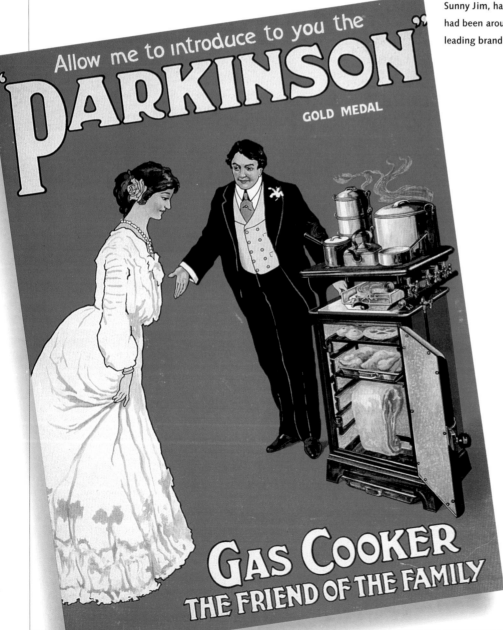

Allow me to introduce to you the "PARKINSON" GOLD MEDAL GAS COOKER THE FRIEND OF THE FAMILY

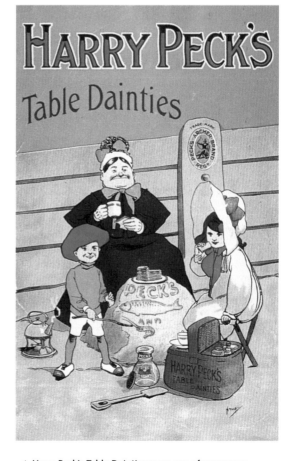

△ Harry Peck's Table Dainties were one of many new delicacies on offer. This advertisement, dating from around 1905, was illustrated by the prolific artist John Hassall, who also created the Skegness poster of 1909 seen on p. 24.

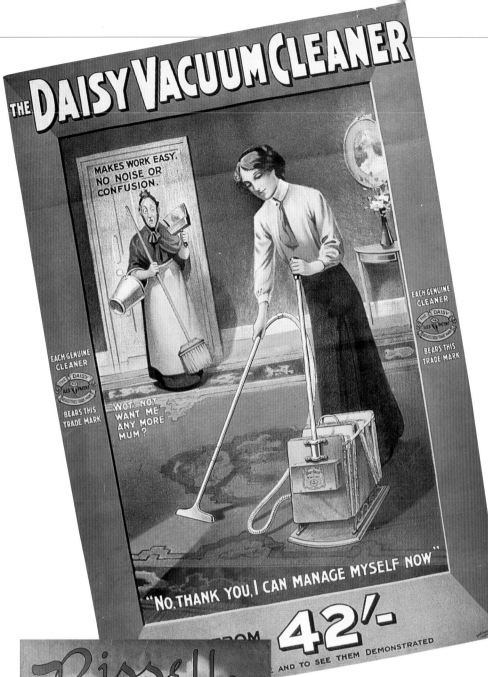

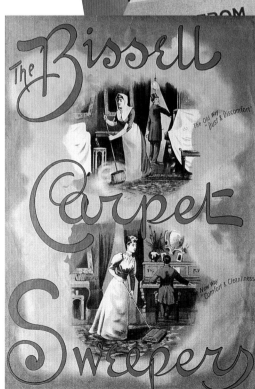

◁△▷ The businessman Hubert Booth had witnessed the failure of railway companies to clean its carriages with compressed air; the resulting dust cloud simply settled again. After forming the British Vacuum Cleaner Company in 1902, he gained royal patronage and provided entertainment at society tea parties with his innovative device. But Booth's machine was cumbersome – the pump that sucked out the dirt was mounted on a horse-drawn van – and at the time most people relied on the Bissell carpet sweeper, patented in 1876. Meanwhile in America, W. H. Hoover was developing an upright vacuum cleaner; this reached Britain in 1912.

Fashion

Fashion was the prerogative of the wealthy, able to follow the latest Paris styles. For ladies this meant yards of lace ruffles and frilly, lingerie-type fabrics. Body shape was dictated by the S-shaped corset which forced the bust forward and pushed the hips back, minimising the waist. Society women of the period would change their outfit as often as four times a day.

High collars were much in evidence for both sexes; Queen Alexandra began this fashion by wearing a choker decorated with pearls. (See also the fashions on pp. 26, 28, 33 and 35.)

▽ Ladies' hats of the Edwardian era displayed a profusion of creativity. Flowers, especially roses, were a favourite adornment, as were feathers.

By the end of the decade, as dresses became less full and flouncy, the hat assumed increasing importance and was frequently worn in the home.

△ The parfumiers of Paris and London vied to create the best fragrance. Packaging was flamboyant, and each bottle of perfume came in its own decorated box. The Art Nouveau style influenced the look of advertisements.

Colman's Starch

Pure and Unadulterated

NOW THAT FATHER'S SHAVED HIS WHISKERS OFF, AND MOTHER WEARS A HAREM SKIRT, HOW CAN I TELL WHICH IS WHICH?

AERTEX CELLULAR

△▷ By the end of the decade a confusing fashion trend was about to begin. Beneath a formal exterior, many an Edwardian gentleman wore Aertex, marketed from 1908.

△▷ Many materials required starching: hot-water starch was used for table linens, curtains, dresses, shirts and blouses; cold-water starch was used for collars and cuffs. The new starch was Robin, launched in 1899 and recommended also as a dry shampoo. Immaculate white outfits were required when smart society wintered in Mediterranean resorts.

COLMAN'S CREAM STARCH

Colman's No 1 RICE Starch GOLD MEDAL

Reckitt's ECRU (CREAM COLOR) Starch

ROBIN The New Starch.

COLMAN'S STARCH

Entertainment

Throughout the 19th century people had been fascinated by a variety of devices, including musical boxes that allowed them to play music without mastering an instrument. The American Thomas Edison is said to have invented the phonograph, which produced music and speech from recordings in the form of metal cylinders in 1877. In 1888 Emil Berliner introduced a device that he called the gramophone, which played flat metal discs. Eight years later a reliable spring-driven motor was added to Berliner's machine, ushering in a new era of recorded music.

△▷ In 1899 the London-based Gramophone Company purchased *His Master's Voice*, painted by Francis Barraud. Originally the terrier, 'Nipper', listened to a phonograph, but this was altered to show the gramophone and became the company's trade mark. The machine above dates from 1902. The Polyphon (right) dates from the turn of the century. A penny in the slot would play a tune from a large metal disc.

RINK BISCUITS

PEE

◁▽ Roller-skating, which had been introduced from America in the early 1870s, reached the height of its popularity in Britain between 1906 and 1912, by which time rinks were in operation all over the country. Rink Biscuits, made by Peek Frean, were marketed to capitalise on the pastime's growing appeal when they were launched around 1908.

Group XIII No 35.   Price 6d Nett.

SPALDING'S
ATHLETIC LIBRARY

Roller Skating
Guide

BRITISH SPORTS PUBLISHING COMPANY Ltd.
2&3, Hind Court, Fleet Street, London, E.C.

RINKING

"MY STYLE IS CAUSING A SENSATION!"

DON'T GO DRINKING WHEN YOU'RE RINKING

Collins's
ISLINGTON GREEN, N.
STALLS

CHARLEY'S AUNT

"FLYING NOW BUT STILL RUNNING"

▷ For many, the theatre was an important social event. Posters for shows at this time were colourful and sometimes topical. The big success was J. M. Barrie's *Peter Pan*. First produced in London in 1904, it received sufficient acclaim to open in New York the following year. *Charley's Aunt*, produced by Brandon Thomas in 1892, ran for 1,466 shows.

33

Communications

In Edwardian times the telephone service was still in its infancy, although the network was growing gradually. The latest advance in communications was wireless telegraphy – the transmission of radio signals by Morse code. The system was pioneered by the Italian inventor Guglielmo Marconi, who sent Morse signals across the Atlantic in 1901. In 1907 a transatlantic wireless service was set up.

For the ordinary person, the picture postcard costing ½d provided the cheapest form of communication. It was also fast enough for most purposes – a postcard could be posted in the morning and arrive in the afternoon of the same day. Plain postcards had been in use since 1870 and the picture postcard since 1894. But it was only from 1902 that the message could be written on the same side as the address, allowing the picture to fill the other side of the card. As a result, the comic seaside postcard, with its bawdy humour, came into being. Foremost among the artists specialising in this area was Donald McGill, who drew some 12,000 comic scenes.

▷▽ In 1901 Kodak's Brownie camera became available in Britain at a price of 5s. It was aimed at children: 'easily operated by any schoolboy or girl'. The original Kodak camera was launched by George Eastman in 1888 for use by detectives. This booklet of 1904 lists 17 different Kodak models, seemingly good enough to take pictures at speed.

◁▷ A telephone network had been spreading across Britain since 1878, but even in the Edwardian era the service was restricted to businesses and the well-off. The lady of the house (right) calls the exchange to be connected to Harrods. The first dial telephone exchange came into operation in 1912, but it was not until 1976 that the whole country was automated. The Ericsson 'skeleton' telephone (left) was introduced in 1895 and remained in production for over 30 years. Even so, many rejected it because the exposed pieces tarnished and one's fingers could become trapped.

◁ Sending and collecting picture postcards were immensely popular. Postcards reflected every facet of daily life, particularly those of a humorous nature, in which field the leading names were Donald McGill, Louis Wain (a specialist in comic cats) and Tom Browne. Postcards used to promote cars, products and plays were often miniature versions of advertising posters. Some cards were adorned with real hair, while others unfolded to reveal scenes of tourist resorts.

Motoring and aviation

For the wealthy perhaps the most prized status symbol of the era was the motor car. Their horse-carriage drivers now became chauffeurs. Early vehicles were open to the elements, so driver and passengers wrapped up warm in hats, fur coats, goggles and gloves. Frequent breakdowns made it essential to carry an extensive toolkit.

Progress in motor engineering was rapid. In 1906 the first Austin car was made and 17 different models had been launched by the end of 1908, with engine sizes ranging from 15hp to 50hp. In 1909 the first 'baby' Austin was born, a single-cylinder 7hp tourer.

Across the Atlantic, the Wright brothers had experimented with motorised flight since 1899, and in 1903 made a series of limited flights. Two years later Wilbur travelled 24 miles by air. In 1909 the French aviator Blériot flew across the Channel from France to England, covering 26 miles in under 37 minutes.

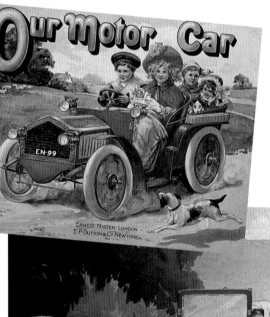

◁△ The widespread interest in motoring was reflected as much by a child's picture book as by royal patronage – the motor car above, carrying the King and Queen, dates from 1904. The Automobile Club of Great Britain was founded in 1897, becoming the Royal Automobile Club in 1907. The Automobile Association started in 1905.

◁△ As the motor car became a more common sight, manufacturers exploited the prestige and excitement of this new form of transport. An 'irresistible' Flor de Varzes cigar is proffered to a policeman taking down particulars, while Bovril was promoted as a sustaining drink for the intrepid motorist.

◁△▷ Aeroplanes of all shapes took to the skies in flying contests. Two early meetings took place at Doncaster and Blackpool in 1909. In 1910 the *Daily Mail* sponsored a London–Manchester air race with a £10,000 prize. Games and books sought to capture the romance and danger of flying.

Toys and games

For children whose parents could afford toys, there was a widening choice of exciting playthings. Notable among them was the cuddly bear. In 1902 Theodore Roosevelt, the President of the USA, created a stir by refusing to shoot a bear cub while on a hunting trip. Morris Michton, an American toy seller, responded by producing a stuffed toy called 'Teddy's bear'. The name stuck, and teddy bears were an immediate success. Within a year the German company Steiff had begun to produce its own version.

Generations of children had enjoyed playing with clockwork boats and trains, but now they wanted toys that reflected the latest inventions – motor cars and aeroplanes. For the lucky few there were even miniature motor cars – which children could actually drive – that came complete with rubber-tyred wheels, headlamps, horns and upholstered seats.

Also in demand were toys that challenged both creative and manual skills, such as Meccano engineering sets and the modelling medium Plasticine (see p. 24). Plasticine was invented by William Harbutt in 1897 for his art students and was first commercially produced in 1900.

△ 'Mechanics Made Easy', created by Frank Hornby, was launched in 1901. After some success he set up Meccano Ltd in 1907. This box dates from 1908, when the original name was being phased out; by now Meccano was available in six progressive sets.

◁ This tin toy car, with its clockwork motor and accompanying engine noise, was made by the German firm Issmayer around 1905. Unusually for the time, the driver was a woman.

◁ Pin the Tail on the Donkey had already been a popular party game for over 20 years when this boxed set was produced. It was still going strong in the 1930s, by which time there also was a version in which the tail could be pinned on to Mickey Mouse.

▷ Although the parlour game of table tennis was played as early as the 1890s, it was not until early in the new century that the craze swept Britain and then the world. Often called Ping Pong – the name comes from the sound of the ball on bat and table – it was a game usually played by adults.

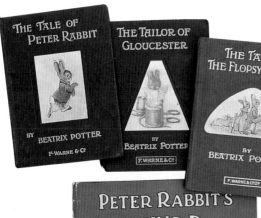
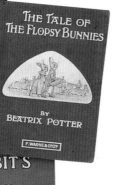

▽ Steiff was established in the 1880s. The German manufacturer's bears shown here date from 1908 and 1909; the larger one has a mechanical arm to allow him to turn somersaults. Steiff did not restrict its output to bears. The British Army officer on the right, with his exaggerated features, is an example of the firm's early character dolls.

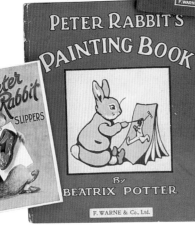

△ Beatrix Potter's *The Tale of Peter Rabbit* was first published in 1901 in a run of just 250 copies. The following year Frederick Warne & Co. published its edition (above top), and the book has remained in print ever since. *The Tailor of Gloucester* appeared in 1903 and *The Tale of the Flopsy Bunnies* in 1909, with others in between. Potter's characters have been used to sell many products, including painting books and slippers.

The 1910s

The early years of George V's reign were full of unrest. The struggle for women's suffrage became increasingly violent, while in places like Liverpool workers' rioting and strikes were at their worst and the army were called out to keep the peace. 'Trouble at mill' accelerated when 300,000 cotton workers were locked out in dispute with their employers. Meanwhile a battle with London anarchists had reached a climax with the siege of Sidney Street (1911). Ireland too was in uproar as the clamour for home rule intensified.

After the American explorer Robert Peary reached the North Pole in 1909, the race was on for the South Pole. A Norwegian, Roald Amundsen, just beat Captain Scott in December 1911, a journey from which Scott never returned. The next year a major disaster struck when the 'unsinkable' ocean liner *Titanic* hit an iceberg on her maiden voyage and sank; 1,513 passengers and crew died.

The craze for the Tango (and later for jazz) was matched by another for going to the 'flicks'. The public queued to see Charlie Chaplin's latest film *The Tramp* (1915), in which his bowler hat, cane, baggy trousers and outsized shoes would become his trademark. The big names of the early silent movies included Mary Pickford, Gloria Swanson, Ben Turpin and 'Fatty' Arbuckle.

Another American import, the Model T Ford, arrived in 1909. So successful were sales that an assembly plant was established in Manchester in 1911. When, in 1913, the revolutionary moving production line was introduced, 6,000 cars were produced that year, selling for £135. Over 16 million 'Tin Lizzys' were made worldwide by the time the model was replaced in 1927.

In 1914 an assassination in Sarajevo escalated into 'the war to end all wars'. The British liner *Lusitania* was sunk by a German torpedo in 1915, killing 1,195 people, including 128 US citizens. The attack changed the prevailing isolationism in America. Sales of charity flags rocketed as money was raised for the war. Rationing was eventually introduced in 1918, but the war was soon over. However, an influenza epidemic was by now sweeping the world. It cost twenty million lives – many more than the eight and a half million lost in the war itself.

Events

World War I aside, perhaps the most important development of this period was the struggle for women's emancipation. This had begun in the nineteenth century, and in 1866 the first petition to Parliament was drawn up in support of women's right to vote. In 1903 Emmeline Pankhurst founded the Women's Social and Political Union in Manchester. The women's suffrage movement became increasingly militant, but with the outbreak of war in 1914 women backed the war effort, demonstrating their ability to do many types of work previously carried out by men. In 1918 the Representation of the People Act gave the vote to women over the age of 30, and ten years later all women over 21 could vote.

△ Biscuit and sweet tins, mugs and decorative books all played their part in the celebration of royal occasions. It was not unusual for manufacturers, in this instance Camp Coffee, to link their products with an event such as a coronation.

◁ The struggle of Irish nationalists to free their country from British rule culminated in full-scale rebellion in April 1916. The Easter Rising claimed more than 1300 lives and initiated a period of armed conflict which was partially resolved by the creation in 1921 of the Irish Free State.

◁ The campaign to secure women's right to vote inspired numerous comic postcards for and against the movement (see also p. 24), as well as souvenir programmes (c.1910) and dance music for Suffragettes (1913).

▽ With the Scout movement well established – there were 150,000 members by 1914 – scouting games and publications were a common sight. Most Scout troops spread the word by producing their own magazine, however rudimentary.

House and home

Mock-Tudor homes were the aspiration at this time – the Ideal Home Exhibition of 1910 featured a complete Tudor Village – and the appeal of this style of building continued well into the 1930s. Inside the home, lighter colours and less imposing furniture were coming into favour. Those with more avant-garde ideas preferred the architectural style of the Arts and Crafts movement.

Ebenezer Howard, appalled by the overcrowding and unhealthy conditions spawned by the haphazard growth of towns, had written in 1898 a book called *Tomorrow* (republished as *Garden Cities of Tomorrow* in 1902). In 1903 First Garden City Ltd was formed and a new town was laid out at Letchworth, within easy reach of London by rail. Welwyn Garden City, also in Hertfordshire, was founded in 1919 and opened in 1922. The availability of comfortable homes that combined the benefits of urban and rural living initiated the age of suburbia and the commuter.

◁ Many attempts had been made to perfect a fountain pen. An American, Lewis Waterman, succeeded in 1884 and from Edwardian times fountain pens grew increasingly popular. Swans and Watermans were brand leaders at the time.

△ The new cookers could also heat bath water economically – a welcome versatility when the requirements of modern life 'have rendered an ever ready supply of hot water a necessity'.

▷ One of the first successful sewing machines for domestic use was produced in the USA by Isaac Singer in the late 1850s. By the end of the century manual sewing machines were available all over the world. It was not until the 1920s that electric models started to make their mark.

△ At a time when electricity in the home was still a novelty, electric lighting became a source of considerable pride. Gas lighting produced an odour and oil lamps needed maintaining. Electricity, clean and easy to use, was here to stay.

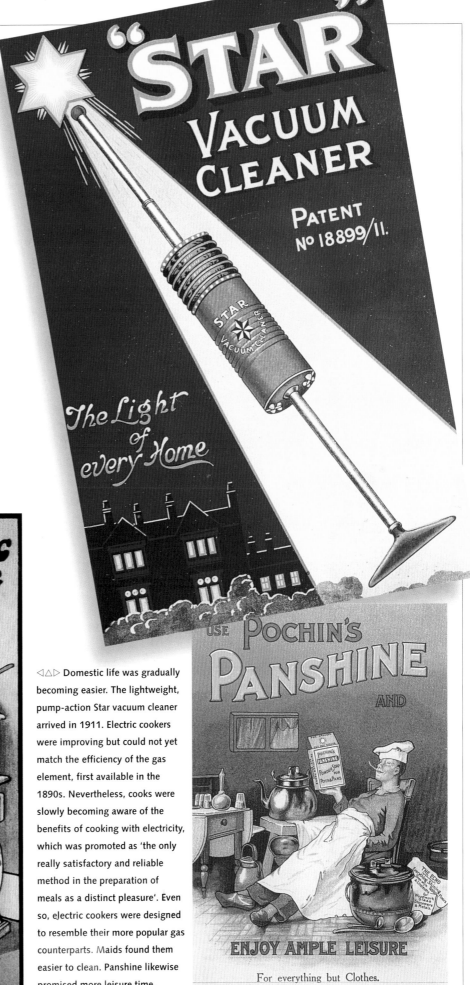

"STAR" VACUUM CLEANER

PATENT No 18899/11.

The Light of every Home

USE POCHIN'S PANSHINE AND

ENJOY AMPLE LEISURE

For everything but Clothes.

ELECTRIC COOKING

◁◁▷ Domestic life was gradually becoming easier. The lightweight, pump-action Star vacuum cleaner arrived in 1911. Electric cookers were improving but could not yet match the efficiency of the gas element, first available in the 1890s. Nevertheless, cooks were slowly becoming aware of the benefits of cooking with electricity, which was promoted as 'the only really satisfactory and reliable method in the preparation of meals as a distinct pleasure'. Even so, electric cookers were designed to resemble their more popular gas counterparts. Maids found them easier to clean. Panshine likewise promised more leisure time.

Shops and shopping

The chain store had been a growing part of the retail trade for some time. Sainsbury's grocery shops, for example, increased from just three in the 1880s to 47 by 1900 and 109 by 1910. Among the many other chains was the International Stores network, which by 1912 comprised 380 shops throughout Britain, each with a mission 'to bring the actual producer and the customer into direct contact'. Boots the Chemist boasted more than 600 outlets in 1910, and by 1914 Marks & Spencer had opened 140 branches. However, most marked was the success of the Co-operative Wholesale Society, which by that same year was running over 5500 grocery shops.

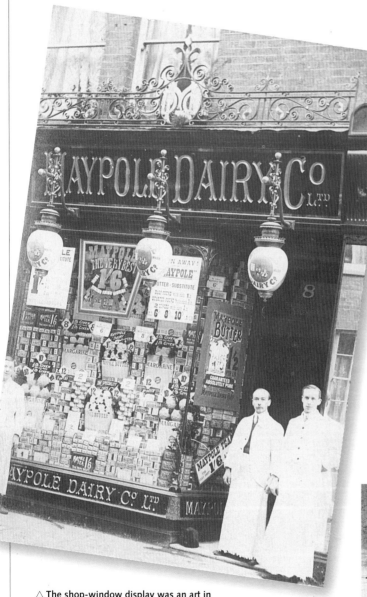

▽ Most products were supplied to the grocer in sturdy wooden boxes. Children made these into carts, while orators found the soap box especially good for standing on to speak.

△ Shops took great pride in the quality of the service they offered. Customers buying groceries, for example, were invited to take a seat while the numerous staff completed their order.

△ The shop-window display was an art in itself, and manufacturers offered prizes to encourage bigger and better exposure of their goods. On winter afternoons huge exterior lamps flooded the window display with light.

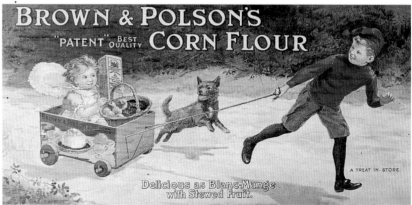

△ Restorative tonics had been much favoured since the 1880s. The makers of Wincarnis claimed that, by enriching the blood, their tonic helped those suffering from malnutrition, nerves, debility, influenza, brain-fag and anaemia. For all such complaints it offered 'a delightful and delicious remedy'.

◁ On foot or on a bicycle, the errand boy was an indispensable part of the delivery service provided by shops. Lyle's Golden Syrup went on sale in 1885 bearing the lion and bees trade mark and the legend 'out of the strong came forth sweetness'.

▷ At Christmas time shops made fine displays of meat, poultry and dried fruits. Customers were invited to join their Christmas club, and the most favoured would receive a free calendar decorated with a chromolithographic picture, sometimes given away also with the purchase of a pound of tea.

Entertainment and fashion

In complete contrast to the billowing skirts of earlier years, the hobble skirt – so named because it allowed only tiny steps to be taken (see p. 40) – made its appearance in 1910. The fashion could not last long, for in 1913 dancing the Tango became all the rage, and by 1919 the jazz era had started.

The great new form of popular entertainment of this period was the cinema, where silent films were accompanied by a pianist or occasionally an orchestra. At first cinemas were patronized mainly by the working class, but during World War I they began to attract a middle-class audience. As films improved, officers home on leave found in them a brief escape from the pressures of war, and now that the tradition of chaperoning young women was beginning to be relaxed, romance could blossom both on and off the screen.

◁△▽ With the mechanism of the gramophone well advanced, makers focused on the horn. This was made from steel or brass (such as the Morning Glory shape of 1904), but laminated wood, which gave a softer sound quality, was available from 1908.

▷▽ Britain's first purpose-built cinema (or kinema) opened in 1907, but it was from 1909 that the rapid growth in the medium began. Three years later, with some 4000 cinemas in operation throughout the country, the market was almost saturated. The poster for *Gold is Not All* (1913) was unusual for the time in that it named the principal actor.

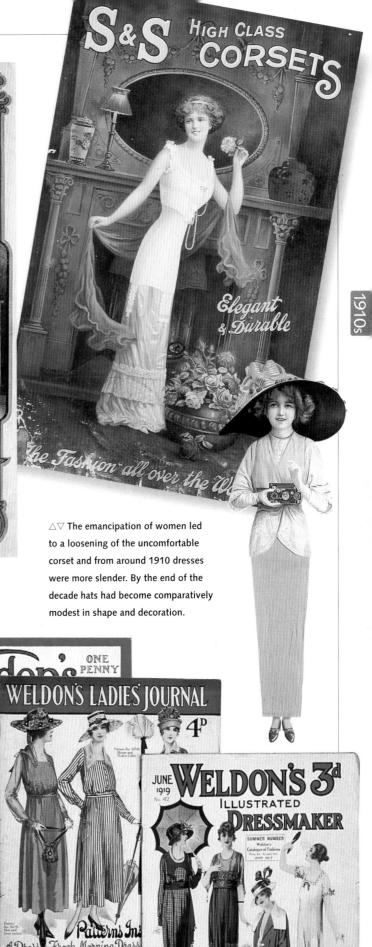

△▽ The emancipation of women led to a loosening of the uncomfortable corset and from around 1910 dresses were more slender. By the end of the decade hats had become comparatively modest in shape and decoration.

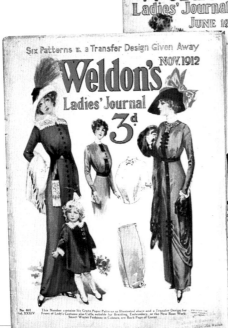

The Great War

A wave of patriotism swept across Britain when the start of World War I was declared on 4 August 1914, and many joined up immediately so as not to miss the experience. The popular belief was that the fighting would be over by Christmas, but Lord Kitchener, who was appointed Secretary of State for War three days after war was declared, could see that the conflict would last much longer. His initial call for 100,000 volunteers was followed by another for a further 500,000. The most famous and much-imitated poster used in his recruitment campaign can be seen on p. 4.

▷ From the outbreak of war, new magazines were published to cover events as they unfolded. Existing titles soon fell into step with the spirit of the times, exhorting their readers to 'send the paper each week to your soldier or sailor boy. It will only take you a few minutes and Tommy and Jack will thank you.'

◁▽ To encourage young men to volunteer for the army, as many as 100 different recruitment posters were issued. The two examples shown here worked on the male mind: one reminded men that their womenfolk were urging them to go to war; the other played on their guilt at not joining up. Conscription began in 1916.

DO YOUR BIT!

SAVE FOOD

◁▽▷ By 1917 there were shortages of food, particularly bread, and from early 1918 meat, butter and margarine were rationed. The role of women on the home front was critical. They took over men's jobs in factories – some of which reportedly doubled production – and on the land, delivered mail and drove buses. As bureaucracy spiralled, many became shorthand typists. Large numbers of women took to wearing trousers while the men were away fighting.

JOHN BULL'S WAR MARCH

Composed by
GEORGE Wᵐ COOK

PRICE 4/=

LONDON.
FRED OLIVER & Cᵒ.   ALFRED OLIVER & Cᵒ.,
OXFORD STREET, W.1

1910s

MARCHING TO VICTORY

EVERY MAN IS NEEDED   EVERY GIRL MUST BE TRAINED

SKERRY'S COLLEGE
RAPID EXPERT PREPARATION

A WOMAN MUST FILL A MAN'S PLACE

WOMEN ARE WORKING DAY & NIGHT TO WIN THE WAR

Y.W.C.A.

£25,000 IMMEDIATELY NEEDED FOR THE WOMEN'S WAR TIME FUND TO PROVIDE REST-ROOMS CANTEENS & HOSTELS

LORD SYDENHAM HON TREASURER   YOUNG WOMEN'S CHRIS...

Wartime toys

The toy industry was quick to produce an imaginative range of board games and puzzles related to the war. Among these were Konskripto, Kapture the Iron Prince, Race to Berlin and the optimistic Air Raid on Berlin, which was 'complete with rules, board, aircraft and bombs'. Many games were inspired by real events. The new game of Jutland (the original version of Battleships) was named after the great naval battle in 1916; Bombarding the Zepps was another game of 1916, based on the raids carried out the previous year by German Zeppelin airships.

The ever-popular jigsaw puzzle was still much in evidence, flying the flag and making heroes of the leaders of the war. Among figures glorified in this way were Sir John French (Commander in Chief Home Forces from late 1915), Admiral Jellicoe (Commander in Chief Grand Fleet, then First Sea Lord) and Lord Kitchener (who was lost at sea when HMS *Hampshire* was sunk in 1916).

◁ A popular game of skill was to manoeuvre a silver ball from one end of a board to the other without letting it fall into the intervening holes. Among the many games based on this idea were The Silver Bullet, Trench Football, How to Get to Berlin and The Way to Constantinople.

▽ From 1916 the image of the tank became a symbol of victory and was pressed into service to encourage the purchase of War Bonds. In 1918 a Tank Week raised £138 million.

△ Chloë Preston's characters, the Peek-A-Boos, had been published since 1910 and were now dressed in khaki, doing their duty in the books and on children's chinaware.

◁ Patriotic board games brought home the reality of war. Running the Blockade, for example, conveyed how the menace of submarines blocked imports into Britain.

▷ The war's most popular comic hero was Bruce Bairnsfather's Old Bill. Serving in France, Bairnsfather's drawings were published in the magazine *Bystander* and then compiled in *Fragments from France*. The first volume sold over 250,000 copies.

On to victory

◁ Writing letters became the vital link with 'Blighty' (home), although censorship was strict. Special field service postcards were issued to troops at the Front (see p. 40).

Yours truly Tom

P.S. Just got the tea

Be sure to send OXO

FROM A CAPTAIN
"You cannot realise what OXO means. Honestly, it may save my life, or at any rate keep me fit and efficient. There is nothing like hot OXO for cold feet or cold tummy either."

FROM ONE OF THE 3RD YORKS & LANCS REGT
"None of the contents of our parcels are more welcome than OXO. Some days we had no bread issue, but we soon learned what a treat it was to have biscuits and OXO."

THE DAILY MIRROR SOMME BATTLE ...RE PROGRESS

△ National newspapers provided extensive coverage of the war. They chose photographs carefully, but it was difficult to hide the 60,000 casualties of the Somme offensive in July 1916.

IT'S A LONG, LONG, WAY TO TIPPERARY; MY HEART'S RIGHT THERE.

THE BARKER AND DOBSON Tipperary Toffee

△ The most popular song of the war, sung by both sides, was *It's a Long, Long Way to Tipperary*.

54

▽ Victory Day was 15 November 1918, when church bells rang out, work stopped and flags were everywhere. There followed a stream of peace mugs and celebratory records.

▷ The Royal Horticultural Society had held the first Chelsea Flower Show in 1913. Now the RHS set up a War Relief fund 'to restore the gardens and orchards of our Allies'.

The 1920s

Recovering from the ravages of World War I, and despite high unemployment, Britain was full of change and invention. Radio provided new entertainment, supported by the advent of the *Radio Times* in 1923 and much 'tweaking of the cat's whisker'. A radical new era in cinema was heralded by *The Jazz Singer* in 1927: the 'talkies' had arrived. The great outdoors beckoned ramblers and cyclists, and with motoring now more affordable, the leisure industry boomed.

Fashions for women changed radically and hemlines rose to reveal more and more leg; the new freedom was advocated by the French designer 'Coco' Chanel. The emancipated woman had short hair and smoked Turkish cigarettes in public. The dance craze from America, the Charleston, arrived in 1925, followed by the Black Bottom. Both were adored by the wild young 'flappers' of the day.

Exploration was still a British pastime. The fabulous treasure of Tutankhamen was discovered by Howard Carter in the Valley of the Kings at Luxor, Egypt, in 1922. The discovery led to a fashion for Egyptian style graphics. In 1924 a British expedition to Everest might have succeeded, but George Mallory ('Why? Because it's there') and Andrew Irving perished near the summit. New speed records were constantly being set for land, rail and air, and the R100 airship was the pride of Britain.

In 1924 the first Labour government took power. Under the leadership of Ramsay MacDonald, eleven cabinet members out of the twenty came from working-class origins. In May 1926 Britain had its first general strike when more than a million workers downed tools in support of the miners' pay dispute. It lasted nine days, during which thousands of volunteers kept services and public transport going.

In the home, housewives aspired to an all-electric house, a fridge and the new Pyrex ovenware. Children loved the books written by A. A. Milne and illustrated by E. H. Shepard. Christopher Robin, Pooh, Piglet, Eeyore, Kanga, Rabbit and Owl appeared in *Winnie-the-Pooh* in 1926 and again in *The House at Pooh Corner* in 1928.

Events

The British Empire Exhibition, which took place at Wembley Stadium over 12 months during 1924 and 1925, was a great success, receiving an estimated 27 million visitors. Among the favourite exhibits was Queen Mary's Dolls' House, designed by the architect Sir Edwin Lutyens, who at this time was also building the splendid Viceroy's House in New Delhi. Manufacturers contributed miniature items, including a working gramophone which played a one-inch record of 'God Save The King'.

The Prince of Wales embarked on many world tours, visiting 45 countries on one trip in 1925. The Duke and Duchess of York also started to make tours.

△▽ Every country of the Empire was represented at the British Empire Exhibition, and some, including India, Canada, Australia and New Zealand, had their own pavilions. Trade and industry played their part; firms issued souvenirs and samples of their produce. Jacobs baked biscuits (see pack below) on site for visitors. The tin above was issued by Rowntree.

The World's most wonderful Exhibition

▽▷ On 27 April 1923 Lady Elizabeth Bowes-Lyon married the Duke of York at Westminster Abbey. Their first child, Princess Elizabeth, was born three years later. Sweet makers created souvenirs to commemorate such events. Marking the visit to Australia in 1927, Hall's Duchess Assortment tin shows HMS *Renown*.

▷ During the 1920s the popularity of the Prince of Wales continued to grow, and his image boosted sales of many products. For the famous portrait on the Rowntree's chocolate box his cigarette was removed from the shot. The box of crackers shows the Prince in his golfing outfit.

House and home

The second half of the 1920s saw a housing boom during which there was a marked interest in smaller houses and flats. These homes were generally modern in style, displaying a touch of art deco in both their outward appearance and their furnishings.

People were influenced by the glamorous lifestyle depicted in Hollywood films, and by the benefits that electricity seemed to offer. The electric kettle, cooker, iron, toaster, coffee percolator, warming plate, electric refrigerator and suction cleaner were appliances that modern housewives aspired to own. As an advertisement for electricity explained: 'The difficulty of obtaining paid help loses its terrors for the over-worked housewife. Electricity is a first-class servant at third-class cost.'

– and so to Bed!

◁△ Feather mattresses were in use until the 1820s, when spring mattresses gradually took over. The Vi-Spring mattress arrived in 1901, and the foam Dunlopillo mattress in 1935.

◁△ During the late 1920s and early 1930s the ideal of a seaside cottage or bungalow was heavily promoted. Popular sites included Peaceheaven and Saltdean near Brighton, and Kinmel Bay on Wales's north coast ('the Welsh Riviera'). 'By making an initial payment of £1 you obtain the opportunity of a lifetime. Come from the city's dirt and grime to sun, sand and scenery.'

◁▷▽ Now that electricity provided the predominant form of lighting, it was convenient to use an electric water heater – 'safety with economy' – although gas was still by far the main source of heat. Some electric fires offered the advantage of being portable (if not particularly safe).

◁ New houses and flats were often designed to include the comforts of central heating, as advertised in this poster of the late 1920s.

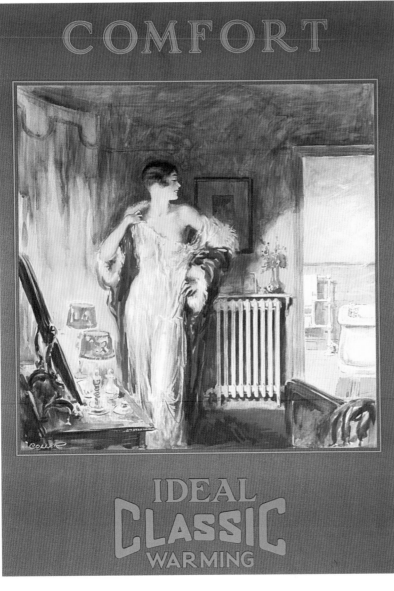

Sweets

The choice of sweets grew substantially during this period. Cadburys had launched its chocolate bars Flake and Fruit & Nut in 1920 and 1921 respectively, and Fry's Crunchie came on to the market in 1929. Confectionery makers responded to the increasing amount of leisure time enjoyed by much of the population with a proliferation of weekend assortments, many of which were sold in attractively decorated tin boxes. Rowntree's Motoring Chocolate was available from 1926 to sustain the motorist with its almonds and raisins.

However, in an age when chocolate was still a luxury, toffee was much in demand to stop the cravings of those with a sweet tooth. At this time toffee was produced by hundreds of small firms, and some of these grew into major concerns; among the biggest companies was that of Edward Sharp, which had installed professional sugar boilers in 1889. Sharp's Super-Kreem appeared in 1919, and was promoted by Sir Kreemy Knut. Mackintosh, which started making toffee in 1890, first sold its Toffee de Luxe in 1917; the picture on the tin shown here is by the children's book illustrator Mabel Lucie Attwell. The firm of Walters was established in 1887 and its Palm toffee was launched in 1922. The Lyons toffee tin of 1929 seen here depicts the ill-fated R101, a British airship which, in October of the following year, crashed and caught fire in France on its way to India.

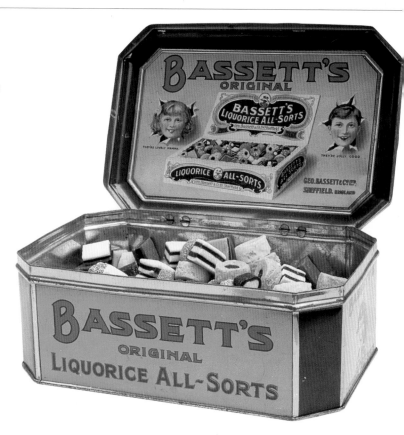

△ Bassett's Liquorice All-Sorts were launched in 1899. The story goes that a salesman accidentally knocked over his box of samples in front of a buyer, who found the resulting mixture enticing.

▷ Individually wrapped chocolate biscuits became popular in the 1920s. Jacob's Club biscuits were launched in 1919 – this advert was designed by W. H. Barriball around 1925.

Fashion

Dramatic developments took place in women's fashions during the 1920s. In mid-decade, hemlines were raised, so that legs went on public show, and women began to have their hair bobbed, shingled or cut back in a severe Eton crop. Such changes in appearance were an eloquent expression of women's new-found freedom.

The close-fitting cloche hat made its appearance in 1924 and soon every woman seemed to be wearing one. Fashions for both men and women became simpler, which led to clothes becoming more affordable. Another result of this trend was that visible class differences began to disappear.

◁ When hemlines rose, sporty women could more easily enjoy vigorous games such as hockey and even take up the racy pursuit of motor cycling.

△▽ Women now felt freer to take up smoking, particularly since the cigarette holder was seen as a fashion accessory. Exotic oriental tobaccos from Turkey and Egypt were favoured.

A Complete Outfit – All Five Patterns inside

LATEST FASHIONS
PRACTICAL PATTERNS

6d

Nov. 1922

£50
for Fashion Photographs
Great Home
Dressmaking Competition
(page 40)

The Most Perfect Patterns made.

THESE 5 Free Patterns Inside

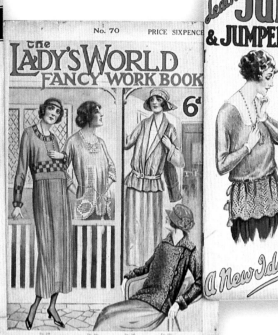

No. 70   PRICE SIXPENCE

The LADY'S WORLD
FANCY WORK BOOK

6d

5 Free Patterns Inside

For descriptions of these Charming Knitted Garments, see pages 1-8.

Leach's # JUMPERS
& JUMPER EDGIN

6D

A New Idea

Weldon's
CATALOGUE OF FASHIONS
AUTUMN & WINTER 1929

6D

THIS FREE PATTERN GIVEN INSIDE   COUPON PATTERN

△▷ Women's dress became less formal, and sweaters became popular with both men and women.

◁ The new energetic dances of the 1920s called for corsets that allowed greater freedom of movement.

▽ Cosmetics were becoming more widely used. Party goers in particular wore mascara, rouge and lipstick made by leading names such as Max Factor of Hollywood, Elizabeth Arden and Helena Rubinstein.

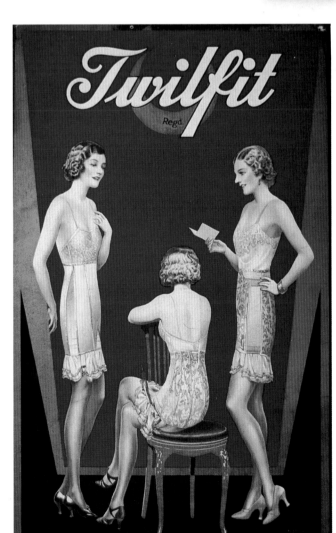

Twilfit
Regd.

MADE IN ENGLAND AND FULLY GUARANTEED

THE ULTIMATE CHOICE OF EVERY SMART WOMAN

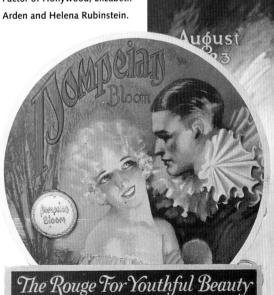

Ladies' Field
EXCLUSIVE FASHIONS

August 1923

PATTERN
OBTAINABLE FREE
WITH COUPON SEE PAGE 48

Pompeian Bloom

Pompeian Bloom

The Rouge For Youthful Beauty

| Light | Medium | Dark | Orange | Oriental |

Radio and film

By the early 1920s a visit to the cinema had become a weekly event for many people, and the faces of the great screen stars were known to millions. A new choice of entertainment opened up for the British public when the radio began to provide daily entertainment. On 14 November 1922 the British Broadcasting Company started transmitting concerts and news from 6pm to 10pm. There was great excitement surrounding this new novelty – within a year of broadcasting there were 500,000 licensed receivers. Listeners were required to buy an annual Broadcast Licence costing ten shillings.

The Radio Times was first published on 28 September 1923; by the end of the decade the programme guide was selling over a million copies a week. In 1924, when the BBC broadcast the official opening of the British Empire Exhibition by George V, more than five million people were thought to have tuned in . Radio images cropped up everywhere – on postcards, china, toffee tins (see p. 63) and games (top right).

▷ The Gecophone wireless was made by the General Electric Co Ltd from 1922. Housed in a mahogany box, this crystal set with a glass-enclosed 'cat's whisker' had an ebonite control, nickel-plated fittings and cost £5 10s. An outdoor aerial and headphones were needed; optional extras were a horn speaker and an amplifier.

The other type of wireless was the battery-driven valve receiver. This was more expensive than the crystal set and its formidable array of dials made it less straightforward to use. However, its advantages were that it could pick up signals from a greater distance and its reception was better.

△▷ Films of the 1920s created great stars such as Lillian Gish, Gladys Cooper and America's sweetheart, Mary Pickford. The heart-throb of the day was Rudolf Valentino; the great comedians were Charlie Chaplin, Buster Keaton and Harold Lloyd. The breakthrough to 'talkies' came in 1927 with *The Jazz Singer*, in which Al Jolson sang a few songs and spoke a few lines. Film magazines and comics featured stars like the seductive Mae Murray (shown top right in typical 'vamp' pose) and the screen siren Louise Brooks, whose bob of ebony hair was widely imitated.

Travel

The first commercial flights carrying passengers had begun in 1919. Then, in 1924, Imperial Airways was formed with the British government's support to offer flights between Britain and major cities in Europe. In 1929 a service was introduced between London and Karachi (at that time in India, now in Pakistan).

In 1923 the privately run railways were restructured to form four companies – LNER, LMS, GWR and Southern – in an attempt to recover lost business in the fields of holiday travel and freight. Meanwhile Britain's roads were filling with cars and commercial vehicles. In 1922 the Austin Seven heralded a new breed of light car for those who wanted mobility at a reasonable price. In that year there were 315,000 cars on the road; two years later there were 482,000. It was as well that petrol stations had been introduced in 1920, for the age of mass motoring had begun.

▽ Air travel was an exciting new experience. In 1924 Air Union planes, each carrying 12 passengers, would leave Croydon Airport at 12.30pm and arrive in Paris at 3pm.

△▽ The image of the railway locomotive was a powerful symbol of efficient travel. The Southern Railway poster dates from 1928 and that for Main Line Flake tobacco from 1925.

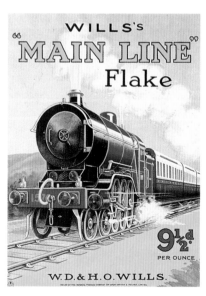

CUNARD LINE

EUROPE AMERICA

YEOWARD LINE
LIVERPOOL

16 Days' Cruise - 21 Guineas
22 Days' Cruise - 30 Guineas
(WITHOUT CHANGE OF STEAMER)

LISBON, MADEIRA, MOROCCO,
CANARY ISLANDS.

◁▽ Even though Alcock and Brown had flown across the Atlantic in 1919 in a Vickers Vimy biplane, the only way for the ordinary traveller to cross the great oceans was by ship. The great liners took five days to steam from Southampton to New York, but comfort rather than speed was the priority. Cunard's *Aquitania* (left) was the world's largest ship when it was launched in 1913. The poster emphasizes the grandeur of this floating hotel which could accommodate 750 in first class, 600 in second and up to 2000 in third. Traditional shipboard pastimes included quoits and bobbing for apples.

Toys

Train sets were a favourite toy for boys. In the early 1920s the German firm of Bing had pioneered small-gauge miniature railways at a reasonable price, but soon trains made by the British company Hornby proved to have greater appeal. After his success with Meccano construction sets, Frank Hornby had moved into toy trains. Although his initial attempt of 1920 lacked finesse, by 1924 Hornby trains running on O-gauge track were setting new standards.

Many games and toys were intended to be instructional and reflect everyday life. For example, the game Safety First! (opposite) made children aware of the growing dangers of motor traffic, and they could play with the latest clockwork car made by Bing (see p. 56).

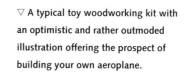

△ Kinsbury, an American manufacturer of toy cars, made models of cars which held the land speed record. The Sunbeam Golden Arrow (above), driven by Henry Segrave, set a new record of 231mph at Daytona Beach, USA, in 1929. Two years earlier he had broken the record in a different car (see p. 4).

◁ Betty Oxo was produced by Dean's, famed for soft toys. With smart coat and gaiter leggings typical of the late 1920s, she was offered by Oxo in exchange for 480 Oxo cube wrappers.

▽ A typical toy woodworking kit with an optimistic and rather outmoded illustration offering the prospect of building your own aeroplane.

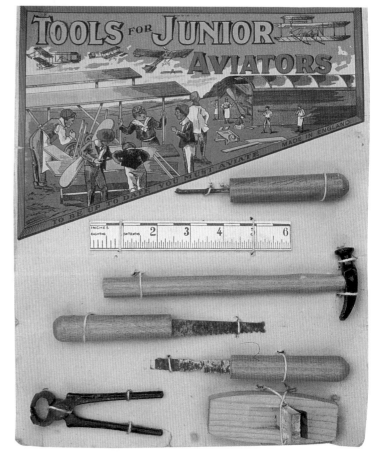

△ This aeronautical board game dates from the late 1920s. Light aircraft were now used for pleasure and flying clubs were being set up. De Havilland's Gipsy Moth was a favourite plane.

△ *Meccano Magazine* had begun in 1916. It encouraged children to build more enterprising models through its competitions, but the magazine was mainly devoted to information on engineering achievements.

▷Made in Germany by Recknagel, this doll has a jointed wood and composition body with sprayed bisque head, blue glass eyes and mohair wig. She wears the latest outfit of 1925.

◁▽ A boxed Hornby No1 Tank Goods Set (costing 21s) and an LNER Hornby No1 Tank Loco (12s 6d), with its embossed box and winding key, are shown with the first *Hornby Book of Trains*, published in 1925.

Children's characters

Daily newspapers were constantly seeking new promotional ploys. One such ploy was the comic strip, whose success was consolidated in the 1920s and which featured an array of characters, many of whom were to achieve lasting fame. Teddy Tail had been in the *Daily Mail* since 1915, and in competition the *Daily Herald* introduced a comic strip featuring Bobby Bear around 1919 (see p. 92) and the *Daily Express* launched Rupert Bear in 1920. The *Daily Mirror* had introduced the highly successful Pip, Squeak and Wilfred in 1919, and the *Daily Sketch* responded by publishing a children's supplement, the *Oojah Paper*, starring an elephant (see p. 92).

The more adult strip Pop started in the *Daily Sketch* in 1921. 'The Adventures of the Noah Family' began in the *Daily News* in 1919, but transferred to the *News Chronicle* in 1930 (see p. 92). Tiger Tim first appeared in 1904 in the *Daily Mirror*, but the characters moved to *The Monthly Playbox* that same year and in 1914 to *The Rainbow*.

△ Dismal Desmond was a creation of Dean's Rag Book Co. in the 1920s and, like Bonzo, was used in advertisements.

▽ The adventures of Pip, Squeak and Wilfred appeared in a comic strip in the *Daily Mirror* from 1919 to 1953. The stories were told by Uncle Dick (Bertram Lamb) and illustrated by Austin Payne. From 1921 the characters were given their own comic supplement; a range of toys followed and, in 1925, the first annual.

▷ George Studdy started developing a cheeky dog in 1912 and by 1920 was supplying full-page illustrations of the character to the weekly magazine *The Sketch*. In 1922 the dog was named Bonzo and remained a favourite throughout the 1920s and 1930s, appearing on postcards, games and Christmas crackers.

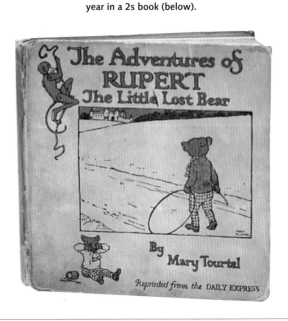

▽ On 8 November 1920 Mary Toutell's creation Rupert Bear first appeared in the *Daily Express*. Rupert's appealing adventures were issued the following year in a 2s book (below).

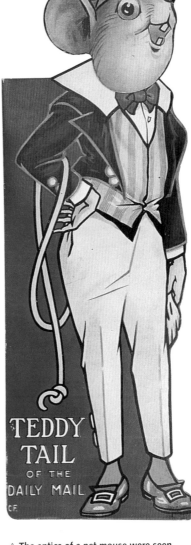

△ The *Daily Sketch* introduced in 1921 a cartoon strip featuring Pop, a good-humoured man who over time lost his hair and gained a paunch. The strip was drawn by J. Millar Watt until 1948, when Gordon Hogg replaced him as the artist.

▽ 'The Jolly Adventures of the Bruin Boys' had started in *The Rainbow* comic in 1914. Tiger Tim and his mischievous friends appeared in his first annual in 1922 and many toys and games followed.

△ The antics of a pet mouse were seen in the *Daily Mail* cartoon strip between 1915 and 1960. This was created by the artist Charles Folkard, whose brother Harry followed by Herbert Foxwell later took over the drawing.

△ Felix the Cat was created by Otto Messmer in 1920 and promoted by Pat Sullivan, whose film studio produced 26 cartoons in a single year. Particularly popular in Britain, Felix was the first cartoon character to achieve worldwide appeal.

The 1930s

The Wall Street Crash of 1929 may have seemed far away, but events in America affected Britain more than ever – by 1932 there were three million unemployed. The feeling of gloom was echoed by Aldous Huxley's depressing vision of the future in *Brave New World* (1932) and George Orwell's bleak picture of unemployment in *The Road to Wigan Pier* (1937). The jobless of Jarrow marched on London in 1936, while Oswald Mosley's fascists (formed 1932) caused trouble in the capital.

Nevertheless there was plenty to be cheerful about. The cinema now offered 'talkies'. The special effects in *King Kong* had everyone gasping, while the seven-year-old Shirley Temple was the top box office attraction in 1935, and cigarette cards of film stars were a popular subject to collect. For the kids there were Mickey Mouse and Popeye, and in 1937 the first feature-length cartoon: *Snow White and the Seven Dwarfs*. The word game Lexicon could be found in most homes, but from 1936 it was rivalled by Monopoly. Young children were now lucky enough to have Dinky toys. Good news for readers in 1935 came in the form of the Penguin paperback, which went on sale for 6d. Radio was an established part of daily life, broadcasting news and shows like *The Crazy Gang* and Arthur Askey's *Band Waggon*. Listeners enjoyed the wave of new chocolate bars that swept the sweet shops – Aero, Milky Way, Milky Bar, Kit Kat and Mars bars at 2d.

Labour saving electrical appliances were used in more and more homes. At the beginning of the decade a quarter of houses had access to an electric supply (half by 1939), and by 1934 the national grid was complete. Comparatively few homes had a telephone in 1931 – although telephones were soon available in four colours – but the majority of businessmen were on the 'phone, and for their desks the Anglepoise lamp, designed by George Carwardine, was launched in 1933.

The shock of Edward VIII's abdication was swiftly followed by the rumblings of unrest in Europe, beginning with the civil war in Spain (1936–9). Neville Chamberlain's 'peace for our time' proved to be a false dawn. War was declared on Germany in September 1939.

Royal events

Whatever else was occupying the public's thoughts during the latter half of the 1930s – and the rebirth and rearming of a Germany hungering to avenge its defeat in the First World War was growing ever more apparent – the situation surrounding the abdication of Edward VIII became a national debate.

The decade had begun quietly; George V decided to make economies in the royal family's lifestyle to reflect the nation's hardship that had resulted from the worldwide economic depression. The King made his first Christmas broadcast to the Empire in 1932, and in the following year he watched his first moving picture, a Walt Disney cartoon. The Silver Jubilee in 1935 was heralded by church bells ringing, fireworks and street parties throughout the country. However, in January 1936 George V died, and he was succeeded by the Prince of Wales, who became Edward VIII on his accession.

Unknown to most of his subjects, King Edward dearly wished to marry Mrs Simpson, a divorcee. In December 1936 he took the unprecedented step of abdicating so that he could do so, and his brother, the Duke of York, succeeded him to the throne as George VI. Shy and afflicted with a stammer, which he strove to overcome, the new monarch nevertheless had determination and the unflagging support of his wife, Queen Elizabeth.

△ The two princesses became the darlings of the nation. Margaret was born in 1930, joining her four-year-old sister Elizabeth.

▽ King George's Silver Jubilee took place on 6 May 1935. Souvenirs of the much-loved monarch's 25-year reign were to be seen everywhere.

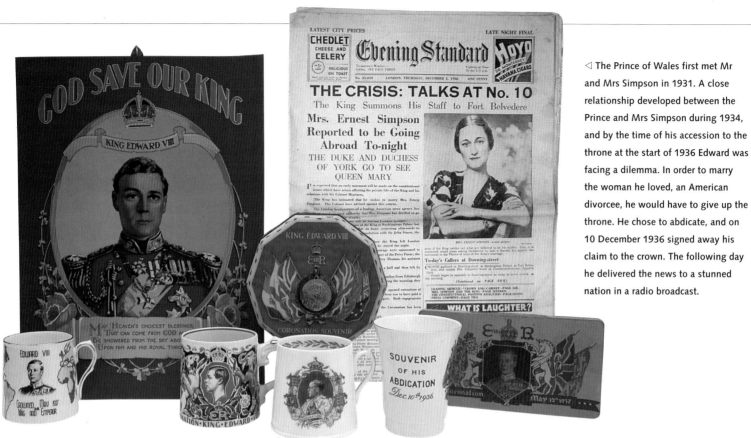

GOD SAVE OUR KING

KING EDWARD VIII

May Heaven's choicest blessings,
That can come from GOD above,
Be showered from the sky above
Upon him and his royal throne.

KING EDWARD VIII
CORONATION SOUVENIR

Evening Standard

LATEST CITY PRICES
CHEDLET CHEESE AND CELERY

LATE NIGHT FINAL

No. 35,030   LONDON, THURSDAY, DECEMBER 3, 1936   ONE PENNY

THE CRISIS: TALKS AT No. 10

The King Summons His Staff to Fort Belvedere

Mrs. Ernest Simpson Reported to be Going Abroad To-night

THE DUKE AND DUCHESS OF YORK GO TO SEE QUEEN MARY

WHAT IS LAUGHTER?

SOUVENIR OF HIS ABDICATION Dec. 10th 1936.

⊲ The Prince of Wales first met Mr and Mrs Simpson in 1931. A close relationship developed between the Prince and Mrs Simpson during 1934, and by the time of his accession to the throne at the start of 1936 Edward was facing a dilemma. In order to marry the woman he loved, an American divorcee, he would have to give up the throne. He chose to abdicate, and on 10 December 1936 signed away his claim to the crown. The following day he delivered the news to a stunned nation in a radio broadcast.

▷ The date for the coronation was set for 12 May 1937, but it was not to be Edward VIII's. Following his abdication, the date remained the same, but it was the Duke of York who took the crown. Souvenirs for Edward had, in the main, been produced before his abdication; among these was the ornate mug above, designed by Dame Laura Knight. Now a completely new range of rosettes, bunting and other memorabilia was required.

KING GEORGE VI CORONATION FAVOUR

THE CORONATION BANDEAU

1937 CORONATION SOUVENIR

House and home

In response to the continuing decline in the use of domestic staff, manufacturers produced a steadily improving selection of labour-saving appliances for the home. Advertisements showed the smiling housewife with her 'all British' Vactric or Cannon gas cooker with Autimo control.

Nevertheless, plenty of families still employed a maid, who wore the traditional uniform, including apron and cap, and served a formal afternoon tea, complete with sandwiches and cakes. Nannies pushing prams around the park were still a familiar sight.

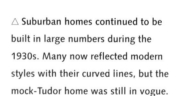

△ Suburban homes continued to be built in large numbers during the 1930s. Many now reflected modern styles with their curved lines, but the mock-Tudor home was still in vogue.

◁ Much importance was attached to the manageable garden with its trimmed lawn and neat flower-beds. This brought the healthy feel of the countryside right to the front door. Part-time gardeners were still widely employed, but lawnmowers were advertised as being easy enough for the lady of the house to control.

▷ Creams and pastel colours were favoured in the home, and printed fabrics returned in the late 1930s. Notice the Mickey Mouse toys on the floor.

The New "Jubilee" 1910
Model Lights the Way
1920
1930

The HOOVER
It BEATS . . . as it Sweeps . . . as it Cleans

Among the ever-growing range of appliances designed to reduce the housewife's workload was the new Jubilee Hoover, which boasted a novel dust-seeking light. The advertisement for the Ewbank Solent table mangle thoughtfully suggested: 'Talk it over with your husband.'

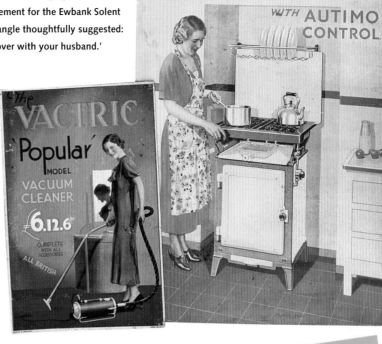

The VACTRIC
'Popular' MODEL
VACUUM CLEANER
£6.12.6
COMPLETE WITH ALL ACCESSORIES
ALL BRITISH

CANNON GAS COOKERS
WITH AUTIMO CONTROL

Mc Vitie's!

The SOLENT TABLE MANGLE
An improved Self-Lifting Machine
Talk it over with your husband
MADE BY Ewbank

Health and hygiene

A greater awareness of bodily and oral hygiene coincided with an increasing standard of living that was to continue throughout the decade. More people could afford the new toilet soaps, and growing competition between manufacturers brought prices down – for example, a bar of soap that cost 4½d in 1930 had dropped in price to 3d by 1935. Similarly, toothpaste in tubes became cheaper, so that even those on modest incomes were now using it regularly, whereas before many had used tooth powders. For children, the favourite toothpaste was Gibbs Dentifrice, which came as a compact pink block in an aluminium tin. This product had been widely promoted since the 1920s as being the 'defenders of the Ivory Castles', fighting off Giant Decay.

A growing public understanding of vitamins, nutrition and diet led the healthy-minded and those conscious of their figures to try out new products such as Energen digestive biscuits, which were designed to aid 'sane slimming'.

△ The desire to lose weight prompted strong demand for products like Vita-Weat, Macvita, Dar-Vita and Ryvita crispbread – 'broken into hot milk or soup – never goes mushy like white bread so used'.

◁ Demand for toilet soap and toothpaste continued to grow. Palmolive toilet soap had been available in Britain since 1913, Lux had arrived in 1928 and Lifebuoy was relaunched in 1933, later making people aware of body odour (BO). Tooth powders in tins were seen as old-fashioned – the trend was towards toothpaste in more convenient tubes. Popular brands included Gibbs, Kolynos, Colgate, Macleans and Pepsodent. For men there were creams to keep every hair in place. Launched in 1928, Brylcreem became the most popular.

△ Still bringing sparkle to homes in the 1930s were Harpic (1924), Windolene (1922), Duraglit (1927). Brillo arrived from America in 1928.

▽ Among the countless products competing to take on the weekly wash, one had been developed as the result of extensive research into synthetic or soapless detergents. This was Dreft, a 'new suds discovery' which arrived in 1937 and was subsequently relaunched after the war, in 1948. A wire 'soap saver' (below) allowed the remnants of soap to be whisked around in the hot washing-up water – thrift was still the watchword.

△ Rinso had been launched in 1910, and by the mid-1930s was promoted as a good way to clean greasy plates and dirty cutlery. Oxydol, introduced in 1930 as the complete household soap, 'makes glassware and china sparkling bright and clean'.

Food and drink

More than ever before, children were targeted in food product marketing. The child star Shirley Temple promoted Quaker's Puffed Wheat, announcing 'This is my cereal'. The Dionne quins (born in Canada in 1934, the first quintuplets to survive infancy) appeared on a host of brands worldwide, including Palmolive soap.

While tea had been drunk in Britain since the 18th century, the recognisable brand was a more recent innovation. Typhoo, for instance, had been launched in 1905, and at about the same time Ovaltine, Horlicks and Bournville Cocoa arrived. The major launch in the 1930s was Cadbury's Bourn-Vita, 'the good-night drink that becomes tomorrow's energy'. In 1935 the League of Ovaltineys was born, broadcasting on Radio Luxembourg on Sunday evenings. By the end of the decade there were five million club members.

◁△ Milk was delivered twice a day in bottles sealed with cardboard discs, but in 1935 United Dairies began to seal their bottles with aluminium foil tops. The familiar horse-drawn milk carts, such as the one shown here, could still be seen on the streets until the 1950s, when they were phased out in favour of the electric milk float.

▷▽ In 1934 Cadbury's launched Cococubs, little creatures who were led by a boy called Jonathan. For a few years metal models of the Cococubs were given in each tin of Children's Bournville Cocoa, and their adventures appeared in national newspapers. Many brands used the well-tried recipe of offering free gifts in exchange for coupons.

◁ There was a growing appetite for breakfast cereals in the 1930s. Shredded Wheat had already built a factory in Welwyn Garden City in 1925, and by the end of the 1930s demand was so high for Cornflakes, Rice Krispies and Puffed Wheat that the US companies Kellogg's and Quaker established factories in Britain.

△ In the early 1930s sliced bread was quite a novelty. Lyons were also known for their cakes and pies, pre-packed in cartons for 'purity and freshness'.
▷ The League of Ovaltineys rapidly became a national institution that every child aspired to join – reading the comic, singing the song, learning the secret signs and wearing the badges.

The tuck shop

On every street corner in the 1930s, or so it would seem, there was a confectioner's shop selling newspapers, magazines, cigarettes and sweets to a stream of mainly local customers. Piled high in the window of such a 'sweet shop' would be dummy packs and display cards advertising products, usually confectionery, on sale inside. In the shop shown in the main photograph below, magazines were hung behind the door and a vending machine was available outside when the shop was closed.

Along with a wide choice of new chocolate bars came boxed selections of chocolates. Rowntrees had researched the preferences for those with chocolate centres, and in 1933 launched Black Magic in an Art Deco-style box (which remained unchanged until 1971). Dairy Box and Quality Street followed in 1936 and Cadbury's Roses in 1937. The first popularly priced boxed chocolates were Milk Tray, 'the box for the pocket', introduced back in 1916.

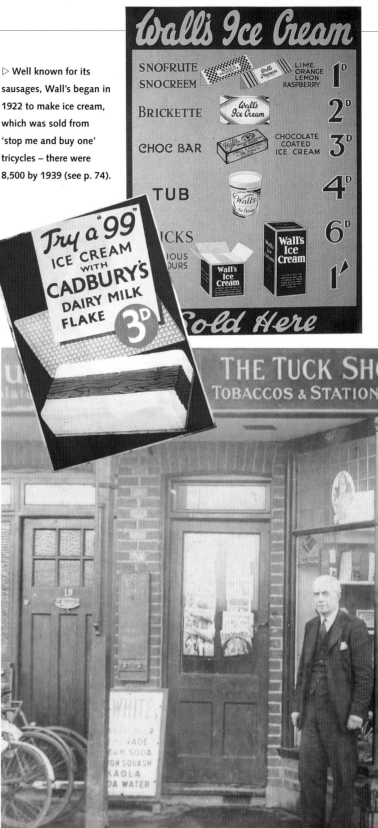

▷ Well known for its sausages, Wall's began in 1922 to make ice cream, which was sold from 'stop me and buy one' tricycles – there were 8,500 by 1939 (see p. 74).

◁ A feast of chocolate bars. Mars arrived on the market in 1932, Cadbury's Whole Nut in 1933, and in 1935 came Aero, Milky Way and Chocolate Crisp. The last was renamed Kit Kat in 1937, the same year that Smarties, Rolo and Nestlé's Milky Bar appeared.

▷ A selection of major cigarette brands of the 1930s. Many of these contained cards that were avidly collected by both smokers and children, who would frequently beg them from adults and trade them among themselves. In the early 1930s a coupon war raged between the tobacco companies, but this ended by mutual agreement in 1933.

▷ More women were now smoking, and smoking more. In 1930 they accounted for five per cent of cigarette sales; by 1939 this figure had doubled. Cork-tipped brands like Craven 'A' – 'will not affect the throat' – were favoured. Du Maurier had launched the first true filter tip in 1929.

Toys and comics

A variety of toys to suit the taste of every child was now available. As well as Frog model aircraft, Lines Bros (founded in 1919) made pedal cars, tricycles, yachts, dolls' houses and prams under the Tri-ang mark, along with Minic vehicles, introduced in 1934.

Hornby continued to produce splendid model trains, miniatures of the famous record-breaking locomotives such as the *Royal Scot*, *Flying Scotsman*, *Golden Arrow* and *Princess Elizabeth*, which could reach speeds of 95mph.

Electric trains became more popular in the 1930s and the Hornby-Dublo system was launched in 1938. Another Hornby success story began in 1933, with the arrival of die-cast vehicles called Meccano Miniatures, which were renamed Dinky Toys the following year (see p. 74).

Children's annuals linked with specific characters had been popular since the 1920s, and for both boys and girls there was also a wide choice of weekly comics, some offering the occasional free gift.

▷ Inspired by weekly comics and daily newspaper strips, children's annuals were a Christmas tradition. Favourite characters were Uncle Oojah (*Daily Sketch*), Bobby Bear (*Daily Herald*), Jolly Jack (*Sunday Dispatch*), Japhet and Happy (*News Chronicle*) and Teddy Tail (*Daily Mail*) – here with futuristic TV set.

△ An extension of the passion for handicraft was the model construction kit, such as those produced by Frog during the 1930s. This kit dates from 1936.

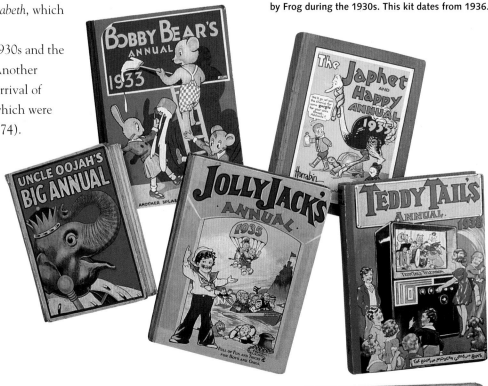

◁ Introduced in 1938, the Hornby-Dublo system set new standards for miniature railways 'where space is limited'. The Hornby catalogue, showing gauge-O train sets, dates from the previous year.

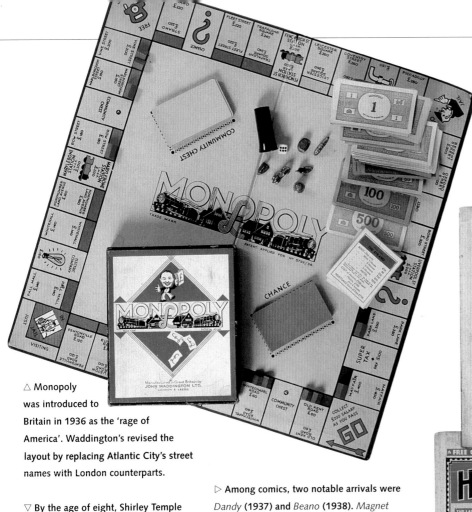

△ Monopoly was introduced to Britain in 1936 as the 'rage of America'. Waddington's revised the layout by replacing Atlantic City's street names with London counterparts.

▽ By the age of eight, Shirley Temple was the biggest box-office draw in the world. In 1934 she starred in five films, famously singing 'On The Good Ship Lollipop' in *Bright Eyes*.

▷ Among comics, two notable arrivals were *Dandy* (1937) and *Beano* (1938). *Magnet* still told the tales of Billy Bunter (introduced in 1908), while the cover of *Modern Boy* celebrated Sir Malcolm Campbell, the holder of world speed records on land and water.

Disney

Cartoons had been popular with children and adults alike since Winsor McCoy's *Gertie the Dinosaur* (1910–19), *Mutt and Jeff* (1916–21), the immensely successful Felix the Cat, who had 'kept on walking' through the 1920s, and the antics of Popeye the Sailor (see p. 74), fortified by his can of spinach during the 1930s.

Before he launched his cartoons, which were to become popular all over the world, Walt Disney and his colleagues worked on a series of films that integrated real people and animated drawings. The first, in 1923, was *Alice's Wonderland*, and a further 56 Alice comedies followed. In 1927 a lucky rabbit, Oswald, was featured in 26 cartoons, and the following year saw the release of *Steamboat Willie*, starring Mickey Mouse (and also Minnie Mouse). This was the first animated movie with properly synchronized sound, and it became an instant success. More characters followed: Clarabelle Cow (1928), Horsecollar Horace (1929), Pluto (1930, but only named from 1931), Goofy (1932), Donald Duck and Clara Cluck (both 1934). Disney's *Snow White and the Seven Dwarfs* (1937) was the first of his many full-length coloured animated films.

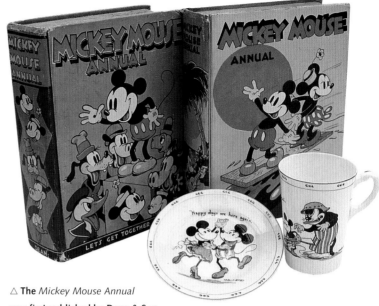

△ The *Mickey Mouse Annual* was first published by Dean & Son in 1931. Paragon of Staffordshire produced the chinaware.

△◁ The *Silly Symphony* film series, which started in 1929, spawned many Disney characters, including Donald Duck, who appeared in *The Wise Little Hen* of 1934. From 1937, Donald was given his own series of short films. These established his irascible nature, but he was still lovable enough to inspire toys made from fabrics, tin (with clockwork) and celluloid. The early Donald Duck had a longer beak. Donald has now appeared in more films than Mickey Mouse.

▽ The toy lantern outfit showed many of the *Silly Symphony* stories, including the greatest success of the series, *The Three Little Pigs* (1933), which captivated children with the song 'Who's Afraid of the Big Bad Wolf?'

△▷ By 1939 there were about 100 cartoons featuring Mickey Mouse, inspiring a never-ending stream of books, soft toys and games. Mickey was also used to promote such products as Price's night lights and Sharp's toffee (see p. 74). The clockwork tail of Pluto rolled him over.

▽ *Snow White and the Seven Dwarfs* was the first full-length animated film in colour. The sensation of 1937, it made both the dwarfs – Bashful, Grumpy, Sleepy, Sneezy, Happy, Dopey and Doc – and their songs, such as *Whistle While you Work*, extremely popular. (*Snow White* was the first film to have its own soundtrack album.) The toys were made from a wide variety of materials, including soap and celluloid (see p. 4).

Magazines

Of the many new magazines published in the 1930s, three became significant. *Woman's Own* made its debut in 1932 using a photographic cover image. It was relaunched five years later with more colour and an illustrated cover to match that of its new rival, *Woman*. In 1938 the revolutionary *Picture Post* was launched; it gave a vivid insight into daily life through its stark black and white photographs, some of which became famous. Previously established picture magazines – for example, *Weekly Illustrated* and the *Illustrated London News* – covered news items in a more restrained manner.

△ The readership of women's and other magazines grew rapidly over the decade and colourful covers were important to catch the eye. *Woman* had gained a readership of half a million within six months of its launch in 1937. Priced 2d, the magazine provided the well-proven formula of romantic short stories and expert opinion on beauty, fashion, childcare, housekeeping and cookery.

◁ Fred Perry well deserved the cover of *Weekly Illustrated*. After taking the Men's Singles title at Wimbledon in 1934, 1935 and 1936, he went on to become the first foreigner to win America's championship outright.

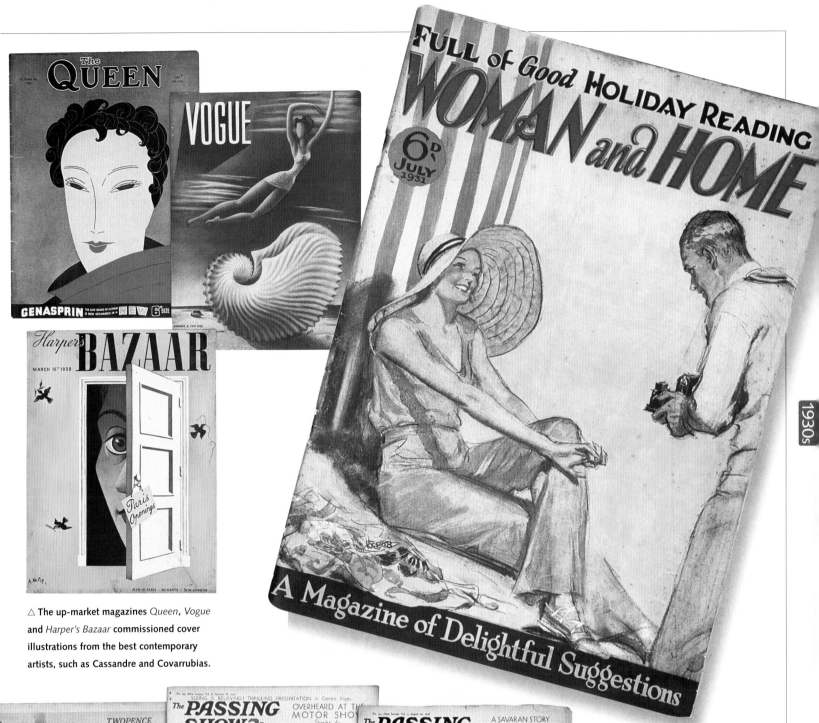

△ The up-market magazines *Queen*, *Vogue* and *Harper's Bazaar* commissioned cover illustrations from the best contemporary artists, such as Cassandre and Covarrubias.

◁ *The Passing Show* was launched in 1915 and by the 1930s had gained a colour cover which made a humorous visual comment on life each week: the fashions, the leisure pursuits or the choice of car, which had all now become lifestyle indicators. A male voice overheard at the Motor Show: 'I still prefer my old short-chassis tourer with its big four engine and its tough, dilapidated body to any of your super streamlined cars.' Companion: 'That's all very well, but I am sure your wife is looking for something more in keeping with modern motoring.'

Fashion

With the number of clothes shops increasing and prices coming down, the era of mass-produced fashion had arrived. The fashionable dress, with a style dictated by Paris, had become more streamlined but could be easily copied. Indeed there was a growing interest in home dressmaking, encouraged by patterns printed in magazines such as *Weldons*, *Bestway*, *Mabs* and *Leach*.

The new development in fabrics was rayon, a synthetic material that was cheaper than many others, although at first it did not prove at all popular. However, gradually garments such as sweaters, jerseys and stockings became acceptable in rayon as the quality of the fabric improved.

The latest tailoring technology enabled most men to afford a made-to-measure suit. Leading this revolution was Montague Burton, 'the world's largest tailoring organization', famed for its suits said to have a five-guinea look but which it offered at 45s.

△ Previously associated with manual labour, a suntan in the early 1930s reflected the image of health, sport and Hollywood glamour. Sun lotions and sunglasses were now high on the fashionable person's shopping list.

▽ Much in vogue were ladies' shoes made from lizard and snake skin, mainly Java python or karung. Also coming into fashion were toeless beach or bathing sandals, some of which were made of rubber.

◁ Tennis was growing in popularity as a social occasion where for many the elegance of the outfit was more important than winning the game. The tennis racket itself had become a fashion accessory.

▽ Shorter skirts increased the demand for stockings and led to a thriving hosiery trade. The CWS (or Co-op), who made these stockings, accounted for a third of all clothes sold.

▽ The powerful influence of magazines and the glamour of Hollywood were a double incentive for women to keep in step with fashion. The most economic way to do this was to make it yourself, with the help of a pattern.

▷ By the 1930s most women had left behind the restrictive corset, and brassieres were now being designed to uplift and shape the female form. In 1935 cup sizes for brassieres were introduced.

Leisure and holidays

Most homes had a radio by the end of the decade, and many families spent their leisure time listening. Radio Rentals had started renting out sets in 1930 and by 1955 had 280,000 subscribers. The BBC provided a programme of news, drama, talks, religion and *Children's Hour*, but most of all music. Popular music was dominated by the 'big band' sounds of Jack Hylton, Henry Hall and Jack Payne. Commercial stations Radio Normandie and Radio Luxembourg invaded the airwaves with sponsored shows such as Gracie Fields from Fairy Soap.

For those who could afford a week's holiday, the seaside beckoned, and holiday camps dotted the coast – about a hundred by the end of the decade. The biggest, run by Butlins, opened at Skegness in 1936 and Clacton-on-Sea in 1938. Each chalet had its own electricity and cold running water, and entertainment was provided whatever the weather. Billy Butlin had built up a string of amusement sites, including, in 1928, the first Dodgem cars in Britain.

BUTLIN'S HOLIDAY CAMP
CLACTON-ON-SEA
IT'S QUICKER BY RAIL
SKEGNESS OR ANY L·N·E·R OFFICE OR AGENCY

◁△ A week at the seaside was an annual event for many families and gave them a chance to escape from the pressures of work. Seaside resorts vied to provide the best facilities and promised more hours of sunshine than their rivals. Most holiday-makers travelled by train, many of which had exciting names like the *Scarborough Flyer* or the *Cornish Riviera Express*.

△ *The Radio Times* **sold up to three million copies a week. Particularly popular were the special editions with stylish covers by artists like Edward Ardizzone, Eric Fraser and Stanley Herbert.**

◁ In the second half of the 1930s new dances were all the rage. Among these was the Lambeth Walk, taken from the production of *Me and My Girl* (1937) starring Lupino Lane (see p. 205) – 350,000 records were sold in six months.

Cinema

Since the 1920s the cinema had provided a refuge from everyday reality, a fantasy world in which dreams could be allowed to live for a brief while. Going to the cinema was all the more exciting because of the magnificent architecture and plush furnishings, often as glamorous as the sets in Busby Berkeley's classic escapist movies.

For many people the stars were the main reason for going to see a film; cinema goers would flock to see the latest offering from the Marx Brothers, for example, whatever the story. However, the 1930s saw some memorable exceptions to this trend, such as *King Kong* (1933), the ultimate monster movie; *The Bride of Frankenstein* (1935), one of the greatest of all horror films; and the cartoon *Snow White and the Seven Dwarfs* (1937), an instant success.

The most famous of all screen romances came at the end of the decade with *Gone With the Wind* (1939), starring Clark Gable and Vivien Leigh.

△ First planned by Howard Hughes as a silent film, *Hell's Angels* was later released as a spectacular talkie in 1930. The classic fairy tale *The Wizard of Oz* was released in 1939 and starred Judy Garland as Dorothy on her travels down the Yellow Brick Road and singing *Over the Rainbow*. Fred Astaire and Ginger Rogers made ten musical films together, including *The Gay Divorcee* (1934), *Top Hat* (1935) and *Shall We Dance* (1937).

▷ A wealth of film magazines kept the big movie stars in the public eye in between releases. Far right: Jean Harlow pours on the charm, Gracie Fields poses with the Blackpool tower, Claudette Colbert wears her Cleopatra costume of 1934. Also seen here, along with Greta Garbo, Marlene Dietrich and Clark Gable, was the outrageous Mae West, who, as Diamond Lou in *She Done Him Wrong* (1933), extended to Cary Grant the immortal invitation: 'Come up some time and see me.'

Picturegoer
The Screen's Most Popular Magazine

No. 385 (New Series), Vol. 8, October 8, 1938.

2d WEEKLY

Errol FLYNN

AN OPEN LETTER TO JEAN HARLOW
PICTUREGOER
2d WEEKLY

◁ While Clark Gable came to represent the essence of masculinity, Errol Flynn was the swashbuckling sex symbol of the 1930s. He was given the lead in *Captain Blood* (1935) and in his most memorable film, *The Adventures of Robin Hood* (1938), where he played opposite Olivia de Havilland.

GRACIE'S PHILOSOPHY OF LIFE
PICTUREGOER
2d WEEKLY
INSIDE 16 PAGE Souvenir Supplement GRACIE FIELDS

1930s

SEX AND SCREEN
PICTUREGOER
2d WEEKLY

MAE WEST *and* CARY GRANT

A Fawcett Publication
Screen Play
Oct. 10¢
10¢

Marlene Dietrich

JOAN BENNETT'S TWO LIVES

What Hollywood *Has Done* to Franchot Tone

GOLD MEDAL SOUVENIR NUMBER
PICTUREGOER

Greta Garbo

Film Weekly 3d.
INTERNATIONAL GUIDE TO FILMS
FRIDAY NOV 2 1934

VARD SUMS UP FIVE FAMOUS DIRECTORS

Motoring

The open road beckoned for many. While public transport provided a cheap day out, the car offered greater independence for those keen to explore the countryside. Between 1930 and 1935 car production in Britain more than doubled, mainly because of small affordable models like the Austin Seven (1922), Morris Minor (1928), Morris Eight (1934) and the Model Y Ford of 1932, the last of which was built at the firm's new Dagenham factory. They were all so different from roadsters like the Humber Ten of 1933 (below).

However, with the rapid rise in car ownership (1.5 million cars by 1935) came an inevitable increase in fatal road accidents. The Highway Code appeared in 1931 and driving tests became compulsory from 1934, the same year that 'Belisha' beacons (named after Leslie Hore-Belisha, the Minister of Transport) were introduced. An urban speed limit of 30mph was also imposed in 1934 and the following year 'cat's eyes' were laid along the middle of roads to make night driving safer.

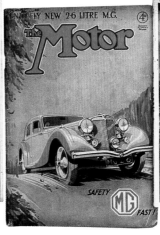

THE TRIUMPH GIL

▷ Underlying a surge of enthusiasm for rambling, or hiking, was the awareness that exercise played an important part in staying healthy. The Youth Hostel Association was formed in 1930, and the following year saw the launch of magazines such as *The Hiker & Camper* and *The Ruc-Sac*. London Underground, whose lines had by now reached leafy suburbia, issued booklets for walkers.

OVALTINE
Concentrated Food
TABLETS

For all Outdoor Occasions

HIKING FOR ALL
By D. FRANCIS MORGAN

6D

△ The motorcycle was a cheaper alternative to the car. Sitting on the pillion, women clung to their man; if there was a sidecar, they could travel more sedately.

▷ Bicycles were mostly used for getting to work, but also 'for the lazy potter through delectable lanes, the evening jaunt or the gay dash to meet friends'. The Women's League of Health and Beauty suggested cycling to keep fit.

◁ Motoring magazines reported on each new car, discussing its engine capacity and comparing models. In addition they gave news of rallies and club meetings, and publicized new road signs. The handsome Wolseley (left) stands in front of the 1938 Scottish Empire Exhibition.

Record-breakers

Since the turn of the century, the desire to go faster, further or higher had grown ever more urgent. Determined men and women applied themselves to setting new records on land, water and in the air. Men like Henry Segrave and Malcolm Campbell, who had battled for the world land speed record in the second half of the 1920s, became the heroes of every schoolboy.

Gruelling solo flights were undertaken by intrepid aviators like Alan Cobham, who flew from Britain to Australia and back in 1926. Charles Lindbergh made his epic flight from New York to Paris in 1927. The first solo east-to-west Atlantic flight was made in 1932 by J. A. Mollison (who married Amy Johnson). The following year an historic flight of over 5,000 miles was made in a Fairey monoplane which retained radio contact throughout the journey. The Schneider Trophy, introduced in 1913, was won in 1932 by a Vickers-Supermarine seaplane which achieved an average speed of 407mph.

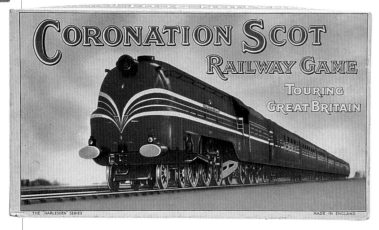

△ The *Coronation Scot*, with its streamlined body, travelled from London to Edinburgh in a record time of six hours in 1937. The *Cheltenham Flyer* achieved 81mph (1932), *Flying Scotsman* 97mph (1934), *Silver Jubilee* 112mph (1935) and *Mallard* 126mph (1938).

▷ In February 1927 Malcolm Campbell had set a world land speed record of 174mph, though this was broken the following month by Henry Segrave with 204mph (see p.4). During the 1930s Campbell went on to set a new record five more times, reaching 301mph in 1935. This tin toy celebrates his February 1931 record of 245mph, set at Daytona, Florida.

◁ The racing circuit at Brooklands drew big crowds to watch the 500-mile races (started in 1929) and the 1,000-mile races (1935).

▷ In a Gypsy Moth, Amy Johnson made her solo flight from Britain to Australia in 1930, the first woman to do so. It took her 19 days to cover 10,000 miles. In 1932 Amelia Earhart was the first woman to make a non-stop solo flight across the Atlantic.

▽ The great ocean liners battled to gain the coveted Blue Riband for the fastest Atlantic crossing. A tussle ensued between the French liner *Normandie* (maiden voyage in 1935) and Britain's *Queen Mary* (1936), which regained the Blue Riband with a crossing of just under four days. The liner *Queen Elizabeth* was launched in 1938 and made her maiden voyage in 1940.

The 1940s

The outbreak of war brought about new attitudes and new values, a community spirit, a feeling that each should do his or her bit towards the war effort – digging for victory, saving on fuel, making do and mending. In the face of great adversities, the phrase was 'keep smiling'.

Children began to be evacuated from the cities in August 1939 and Anderson shelters were distributed in areas likely to be bombed. Everyone had a gas mask and was encouraged to carry it at all times; those for children were given a friendlier, Mickey Mouse appeal. Leaflets, booklets and posters were printed in profusion on all aspects of coping with war on the home front: black outs, air raid precautions, first aid and even how to take care of your civilian respirator (gas mask).

Every part of daily life took on the mantle of war – the cereal supplement Bemax and Mazawattee tea could be bought in gas-proof tins, 'increase your tea ration' claimed a new product call Teafusa, bus tickets and milk bottle tops advised 'raw material is war material' and 'milk for vigour and victory'. Slogans became part of the national diet: 'careless talk costs lives', 'keep mum, she's not so dumb' and 'coughs and sneezes spread diseases'.

The radio became the focus for family entertainment and for the latest news. The popular programme *The Kitchen Front* advised housewives on ways to make the most of their ration – perhaps pea pod soup or stuffed turnips. From June 1941 clothing was rationed, and sweets too, just 3oz per head from July 1942.

As in World War I, women filled the gaps left by the men who had gone to war – as postwomen, munitions workers, air raid wardens, conductors, as well as working for the Land Army to bring in the harvest and tend the cattle. Posters urged women to join the services – such as the WAAF, WRNS and ATS.

The cinema showed a steady stream of morale-boosting movies, and popular songs lifted spirits against a background of blitz and bombing, shortages and salvage. The German U-boat blockade restricted imports, but eventually, the Allied invasion of Europe on D-Day, 6th June 1944, was followed by victory in May 1945. But austerity was worse after the war. Food queues were even longer and prefabricated homes proved a woefully inadequate remedy for the housing shortage.

Wartime reality

It was in 1940 that the reality of war struck home for most Britons. In May Winston Churchill replaced Neville Chamberlain as Prime Minister. At the end of that month and in the first week of June, the stranded troops of the British Expeditionary Force were rescued from Dunkirk. Also in June, Italy joined Germany in the war by launching an attack on France. By this time the Netherlands, Belgium, Denmark, Norway and France had capitulated, and now Britain was bracing itself for the possibility of invasion.

Housewives came to the fore when they were urged by the Ministry of Aircraft Production to hand in everything made from aluminium, including 'cooking utensils of all kinds, bodies and tubes of vacuum cleaners, ornaments and even thimbles'. Their response was overwhelming, but as important as the vital material amassed by this initiative was the psychological boost of bringing a large sector of the population into the war effort.

During August 1940 the Battle of Britain raged in the sky as the RAF's Hurricane and Spitfire pilots confronted the fearsome German Luftwaffe. With the start of the much-expected Blitz on 7 September, Londoners took to their Anderson shelters or the Underground, where over 170,000 people regularly sought refuge.

△ The Home Guard was formed in response to a wireless appeal by the War Minister, Anthony Eden, in May 1940. Within a week 250,000 had joined the Local Defence Volunteers, as the organization was at first known.

▽ For prisoners of war, the food parcel was an eagerly anticipated treat. Each week 2000 Red Cross Volunteers packed and dispatched 90,000 parcels, after tying them with 180 miles of string.

△ The potential disaster of Dunkirk became 'nine days of wonder', as The Radio Times called it a year later. For many, the heroes were those who manned the countless small vessels which crossed the Channel to pick up soldiers.

▽ On 20 August 1940 Churchill paid tribute to the RAF pilots: 'Never in the field of human conflict was so much owed by so many to so few'.

◁ The Blitz on London and other cities, notably Coventry, lasted from September 1940 until May 1941. Nearly 40,000 people were killed, half of them in the capital. As if by a miracle, St Paul's Cathedral survived almost unscathed.

Daily Mail
FOR KING AND EMPIRE
TUESDAY, DECEMBER 31, 1940 — ONE PENNY

LATE WAR NEWS SPECIAL

SHERLEY'S TONIC AND CONDITION POWDERS

Hitler Planned Monday Swoop

London Blaze

WAR'S GREATEST PICTURE: St. Paul's Stands Unharmed in the Midst of the Burning City

America Moves
BIG ARMS FLOW HAS BEGUN

Bluemel's
Cycle Accessories

LET'S GO–

WINGS FOR VICTORY

Lilliput
OCTOBER

With the R·A·F by NOEL MONKS
ILLUSTRATED WITH AUTHENTIC PHOTOGRAPHS

FRY'S COCOA

Rich in nerve food!

THE BALLOON BARRAGE EXPLAINED
NEWNES
PRACTICAL MECHANICS
8D
DECEMBER 1940

WEEKLY ILLUSTRATED
2d

ANTI-AIR RAID: EXCLUSIVE PICTURES

the **GREMLINS**
WALT DISNEY
By Flight Lieutenant Roald Dahl

△ While serving in the RAF in 1942, Roald Dahl wrote *The Gremlins*, about little people who caused trouble. He went on to write such classics as *Charlie and the Chocolate Factory* (1964) and *Revolting Rhymes* (1982).

Austerity

Ration books were issued soon after the start of the war, and by March 1940 bacon, sugar, butter and meat were being rationed on a points system, followed in July by tea. In 1941 jam, cheese, canned foods and other groceries were added to the list of restricted goods. Clothes were rationed from June 1941 and sweets from July 1942. By now almost everything was in short supply, particularly soap, saucepans and toothbrushes. In America it was reported that 'there is a shortage of nearly everything except courage in Britain'.

Families were urged to economize on fuel and electricity by, for example, using only five inches of hot water for a bath and avoiding the use of unnecessary lighting. To simulate stockings, women painted liquid silk on their legs (see right), or even applied Bisto or Oxo, drawing a pencil line for a seam. Propaganda posters urged a wide range of other economies: 'Save fuel to make munitions for battle'; 'Food needs transport, don't waste it'; 'Stop! Think twice before making any trunk calls'.

▽ As shortages in the shops grew more serious, restrictions were also imposed on the use of packaging materials. Paper labels were reduced in size, less printing ink was used and the quality of cardboard became poorer. Everyone was encouraged to save waste paper for the salvage collector, and there was a particularly urgent need for empty bottles and jars. Note the patriotically adorned toilet rolls.

△ Clothes coupons restricted the number of new purchases. The watchword was 'making do' – a practice encouraged by instructive leaflets from Mrs Sew-and-Sew.

▽ Cigarettes were in short supply and from July 1942 sweets were rationed to 3oz per person per week. Blended chocolate contained separated milk, not full cream.

△ The contents of women's handbags reflected the officialdom of war life – identity card, clothes coupons and ration book (at first called a points coupon book). Advice on cooking economically was rife, and included menus for holidays at home.

▽▷ As in World War I, women joined battle on all fronts, playing vital roles as ambulance drivers, air-raid wardens, farm hands and in the Services – ATS, WAAF, WRNS and AFS. *The Gentle Sex* (1943) was a film about seven girls who were conscripted into the ATS (Auxiliary Territorial Service).

Humour

Keeping up morale on the home front was an essential element of the war effort. Central to this task was the radio. Most people listened for the latest war news and comedy programmes such as *ITMA* (*It's That Man Again*) with Tommy Handley. The show's characters, including Colonel Chin-Strap and Mrs Mopp, brightened many a dismal evening. The pre-war show *Band Wagon*, starring 'Big-hearted Arthur' Askey, was revived for a time, and *Hi, Gang!*, with Bebe Daniels, Ben Lyon and Vic Oliver, was another comedy favourite.

Humour helped many people get through the Blitz: a pub offered 'no water, no gas, but good spirits' and a barber's shop next to a bombed-out building announced: 'We've had a close shave. Come and get one yourself.'

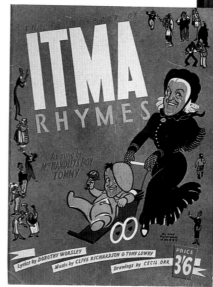

△ Catch-phrases from radio shows became part of everyday language, among them the cry of *ITMA*'s Mrs Mopp: 'Can I do you now, sir?'

△ Postcard humour kept spirits buoyant. Cards celebrating St Valentine's Day, Christmas and birthdays all joined in with topical banter.

◁ Hitler was made fun of at every opportunity. Popular books were parodied to create *Struwwelhitler* and *Adolf in Blunderland*; even Hitler's *Mein Kampf* became *Mein Rampf*. The spoof toilet roll contained sheets showing Hitler: 'Now I'm brownshirt all over'.

▷ Compilations of newspaper cartoons made popular annuals. Giles's cartoons were first published in the *Daily Express* in 1943, and the first Giles annual was published two years later. Nipper appeared in the *Daily Mail* from 1933 until 1946. Jane, with her German 'sausage dog' Fritz, was featured in the *Daily Mirror* from 1932. During the war the saucy heroine spied for Britain. Her exploits were much followed by the troops, and it was reported that she had to be naked to ensure their victory in battle.

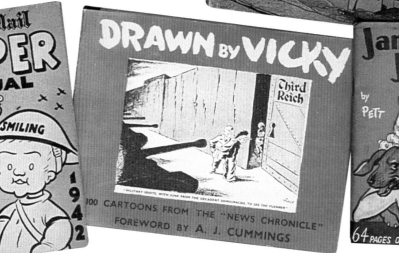

Wartime childhood

For children, life during the war could be both frightening and exciting – in either case it was very different from the comparative calm of the 1930s. Evacuees from the cities found the country a novelty, while for those youngsters who remained in the cities, bombed buildings became playgrounds and looking for shrapnel an engrossing new hobby.

Most toy factories had been turned over to helping the war effort. Lines Bros., for example, switched to making gas masks, tommy guns, ammunition boxes and even scale-model tanks for military training. Games made from card were more economic to produce, but many pre-war toys were handed down, while others were cobbled together from whatever materials were available.

◁▽ Toys, games and puzzles reflected the climate of war. Jigsaws depicted the latest epic battle, and games were based on themes such as air-raid precautions (ARP), Bomber Command, evacuation, the blackout and dressing up in uniforms.

△ Children's books told stories of heroic deeds, and even the unruly schoolboy William did his bit for his country. The creation of Richmal Crompton, William remained an 11-year-old throughout about 40 books published between 1922 and 1970. Percy F. Westerman wrote some 150 adventure stories from 1908 (*A Lad of Grit*) until the 1940s. Biggles was the invention of Captain W. E. Johns, who wrote 102 books on the pilot's wartime flying exploits.

△ Comics embraced wartime themes: aerial exploits, spy mysteries and tales of submarines and unexploded bombs. Younger readers of titles such as *Tiny Tots* and *Rainbow* were exposed less to the reality of war.

▽ Barrage balloons, launched to deter enemy aircraft from flying low, became familiar sights above Britain's cities. Children's story books soon lent a friendly face to such peculiar objects, and aircraft received similar treatment.

Entertainment

The war could be shut out momentarily with the purchase of a 6d seat at the cinema to watch Clark Gable in *Gone with the Wind*, which was released in 1939 and was still being shown the following year. The American film industry produced such classics as *The Grapes of Wrath* and *The Great Dictator* (both 1940), *Citizen Kane* (1941) and *Casablanca* (1942), in which Humphrey Bogart romanced Ingrid Bergman to the tune of *As Time Goes By*. Bob Hope, Bing Crosby and Dorothy Lamour caused record queues at cinemas all over Britain with their *Road to…* series, arriving at Zanzibar in 1941. Disney offered *Pinocchio* and *Fantasia* (both 1940), *Dumbo* (1941) and the classic tear-jerker *Bambi* (1942), which included the delightful comic creation Thumper the rabbit, who for many stole the show. The only thing that could shatter the escapist fantasy of films like these was the inconvenient interruption of an air raid.

In addition to popular morale-boosters such as *Lilli Marlene*, there were plenty of other songs that kept spirits up during the dark days of the war. Many had topical titles: *She's in Love with a Soldier*, *Shine on Victory Moon*, *Till the Lights of London Shine Again*, *Thanks Mr Censor* and *Meet Me in the Blackout, Sweetheart*, the last of these sung by the hugely popular 'Cheeky Chappie', Max Miller.

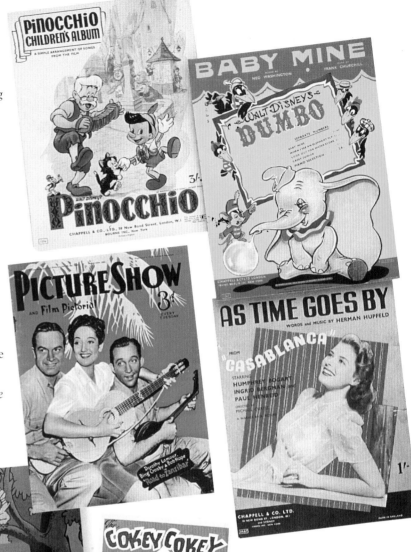

△ Dancing was a popular pastime, and the arrival of American servicemen in Britain increased the passion for the jive and the jitterbug – which inspired the title of Laurel and Hardy's film of 1943.

◁△ Popular songs captured the mood of the moment. The German fortifications opposite the French Maginot Line were nicknamed the Siegfried Line, so it was fun to sing: 'We're gonna hang out the washing on the Siegfried Line.' Sentimental songs such as *We'll Meet Again* (see p. 102) and *The White Cliffs of Dover* made Vera Lynn the 'Forces' Sweetheart'. Potato Pete, whose mission was to encourage housewives to serve more potatoes, also asked them to 'remember to save the water in which potatoes have been boiled, as it is useful as a foundation for a soup'. The answer to *When Can I Have a Banana Again* was 1946.

113

Victory

The road to victory was long and hard, but after nearly six years of global conflict the Allies prevailed. When the war in Europe came to an end on 8 May 1945, Churchill conceded that 'we may allow ourselves a brief period rejoicing'. The struggle in the east still had to be won, but Japan finally surrendered on 14 August. Victory had come at a price: Britain and her Empire had lost more than half a million people in the war. Worldwide it had cost the lives of 55 million, mainly in the Soviet Union, China, Germany and Poland.

On the home front, millions of Britons had survived the years of daily hardship by adopting a practical and frequently enterprising outlook. By 1944 more than a quarter of all fresh eggs were laid by chickens kept in garden sheds, and a million tons of vegetables were being grown on allotments.

Come and help with the VICTORY HARVEST

You are needed in the fields !

APPLY TO NEAREST EMPLOYMENT EXCHANGE FOR LEAFLET & ENROLMENT FORM OR WRITE DIRECT TO THE DEPARTMENT OF AGRICULTURE FOR SCOTLAND 15 GROSVENOR STREET, EDINBURGH.

For a healthy, happy job

Join the WOMEN'S LAND ARMY

CLIVE UPTON

For details: APPLY TO NEAREST W.L.A. COUNTY OFFICE OR TO W.L.A. HEADQUARTERS 6 CHESHAM PLACE LONDON S.W.1

Minister of Labour and National Service

◁△ The Women's Land Army tackled many tasks, including driving tractors and looking after livestock. Town-dwellers responded eagerly to the call of 'Lend A Hand on the Land'. The growing use of tractors in the war allowed farmers to greatly increase the amount of food they produced.

▽ The initial call to 'Grow More Food' was replaced by the more urgent slogan 'Dig for Victory'. Growing your own food became a national obsession, with gardens and parks pressed into service.

DIG FOR VICTORY

"LET US GO FORWARD TOGETHER"

Daily Mail

VICTORY EDITION

VE-DAY—IT'S ALL OVER

The King to speak to Empire: Victorious generals will follow Premier on radio

Joy-day throngs stop traffic
IN NEW YORK

3 POWERS WILL ANNOUNCE GREAT SURRENDER SIMULTANEOUSLY

All Britain stood by for news
How it broke—hour by hour

News Chronicle
LATE LONDON EDITION

"Hiroshima disappeared in cloud, boiling smoke and flame"

PILOT TELLS WHAT HAPPENED WHEN ATOMIC BOMB FELL

Last Allied warning: Yield, or we lay Japan waste

The back room boys

400 Allied planes hit Jap V2 ramps

MORE ATOM BOMBERS READY TO TAKE OFF

World scientists foresee new era

Rockets that may go round the moon

Atlantic traffic in scientists and vital apparatus

△ On 2 May 1945 newspapers carried the headline 'Hitler is Dead'. VE (Victory in Europe) Day was celebrated on 8 May with the start of a two-day national holiday. Throughout Britain there were scenes of unrestrained joy and happiness. In Japan, two atomic bombs were dropped by the Americans: on Hiroshima on 6 August and on Nagasaki three days later.

△ Within days of taking office as Britain's war leader, Churchill used the words 'Let us go forward together'. The doll above is dressed in ATS uniform and looks at Churchill with his ever-present cigar and bulldog countenance.

▽▷ Shortages of materials meant that few victory souvenirs were produced, although mugs were modified in a rudimentary way. Victory parades were delayed until 8 June 1946.

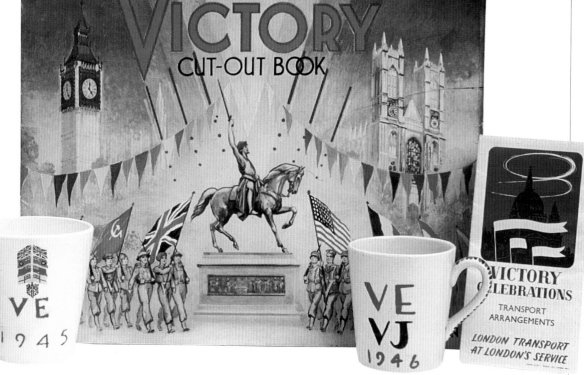

VICTORY CUT-OUT BOOK

V.E. Day
MAY. 8th. 1945

VE 1945

VE VJ 1946

VICTORY CELEBRATIONS
TRANSPORT ARRANGEMENTS
LONDON TRANSPORT AT LONDON'S SERVICE

VICTORY 1945

Post-war events

In September 1946 the Britain Can Make It exhibition opened at London's Victoria and Albert Museum. Reflecting the nation's rapid transition from wartime to peacetime production, it displayed some 6000 products, mostly household goods. However, most of these were destined for export, for it would be necessary to devote a large part of export earnings to repayment of the huge costs of the war and of reconstruction under the Marshall Plan.

The new Labour government of 1945 set out plans to nationalize the gas, electricity, steel and coal industries, the railway and road-haulage systems, ports and civil aviation. Another pressing issue was the shortage of housing. Many homes had been destroyed by enemy bombs, and now demobilized servicemen were swelling the demand for accommodation. Pre-fabricated homes had proved a temporary solution, but the building of council estates continued and new towns such as Crawley and Hemel Hempstead sprang up.

Sport was revitalized, and there were record attendances at events such as motorcycle speedway, greyhound racing, horse racing, cricket and, above all, football; there were 41 million visits to watch matches during the 1948–9 season. Also in 1948, London hosted the first post-war Olympic Games.

△ In 1948 the National Health Service came into being, the National Insurance scheme was introduced and the railway network was nationalised.

△ The Biro went on sale in 1946 at 55s, but gradually the price came down and by 1949 ballpoint pens were outselling fountain pens. It was claimed that a Biro could write 200,000 words without refilling.

▷ John Cobb broke the world land-speed record at Bonneville Salt Flats, USA, in 1947. His Railton Mobil Special reached 394mph – a record that was to stand until 1964.

△ Television returned on 7 June 1946, but the service was limited to a few hours every day, just in the London area. Only about 10,000 people had TV sets, and radio was still dominant. The BBC's Home Service offered news and popular entertainment such as *Saturday Night Theatre*; the Light Programme had *Mrs Dale's Diary*, *Much-Binding-In-The-Marsh*, *Housewives' Choice*, panel games and quizzes. In 1946 the Third Programme was launched for 'the alert and receptive listener'.

▷ An event that captured the hearts of many Britons was the birth of a polar bear on 27 November 1949, the first to be born and survive at London Zoo. The cub was named Brumas; her mother, Ivy, had come from Hanover Zoo in 1947, while her father, Mischa, had been in London since 1935. Dean's Rag Book Co responded rapidly by producing Ivy and Brumas soft toys.

△ Princess Elizabeth married Prince Philip, the Duke of Edinburgh, at Westminster Abbey on 20 November 1947. The couple had first met at the coronation of King George VI and Queen Elizabeth in 1937.

Post-war life

In the second half of the 1940s shortages and rationing were as bad if not worse than they were during the war, and long queues were a fact of everyday life. Bread had not been rationed, but from July 1946 it was for two years, as the result of a worldwide grain shortage.

The Utility Scheme, based on the theory that production costs could be lessened by standardization of goods, had been in place since 1941 for clothes, furniture and household items such as blankets and sheets, and continued until the end of the decade.

Teddy bears were also subject to austerity measures, although Rupert Bear annuals continued to be published throughout the 1940s.

▽ **The Rev. W. Awdry's book** *The Three Railway Engines* **appeared in 1945. The following year he published the story of his most celebrated creation,** *Thomas the Tank Engine*.

△ **The popular radio spy thriller** *Dick Barton* **(starring Noel Johnson) ran from 1947 until 1951. Its memorable theme tune was** *Devil's Galop*.

△ **The first of Enid Blyton's** *Famous Five* **stories appeared in 1942. She had written books for children since 1922 and by the late 1940s was publishing more than 30 titles a year.**

△▷ Christian Dior's 'New Look' was a revelation – romantic full skirts that fell to mid calf. But with material still rationed, such extravagant use of fabric was beyond the means of most people.

◁ In 1947 new post-war car designs appeared: the Austin A40 Devon and the Standard Vanguard with its 'fast-back' body. The Land Rover and new Morris Minor followed in 1948.

▷ More workers now took paid annual leave. After five summers without a holiday, many rediscovered the sandy beaches, at long last cleared of barbed wire. Guests at Butlin's five and Pontin's six holiday camps were reminded to bring their ration books. The bikini arrived in 1946.

Make sure of your place in the sun–by joining a

NATIONAL SAVINGS CLUB

The 1950s

The spirits of the nation were lifted by the Festival of Britain in 1951 and two years later by the Coronation of Elizabeth II. An extra 100,000 television sets were sold to watch the event, and television became the focus of family entertainment. For the youngest children there was a diet of puppets, like Muffin the Mule, Andy Pandy, Rag Tag and Bobtail, the Woodentops and Sooty with his xylophone.

When 'the other channel' was launched in 1955, a whole new innovation was born, watching television commercials. The TV jingles started to lodge in the mind: 'Murray Mints, Murray Mints, too-good-to-hurry-mints' and 'A Double Diamond works wonders, works wonders'. By the end of the decade a third of households had a television set. Many still tuned into the radio though; fans enjoyed *The Goon Show*, with Spike Milligan, Harry Secombe and Peter Sellers, from 1951 to 1959.

Television advertising supported the new types of products appearing in the new self-service stores. Sugar-coated breakfast cereals, tea bags, instant coffee, and an array of bright packs of soap detergents – they made the whites whiter in the electric washing machines owned by half of mothers. The refrigerator, another convenience, was now filling up with frozen foods like fish fingers, launched in 1955.

American culture was having an increasing effect on British life. Marilyn Monroe and Elvis Presley had people pulsating in different ways. Teenagers (a new term that was here to stay) played rock'n'roll on their Dansette players or watched it on the TV show *Six Five Special* that began in 1957. James Dean was the rebel film idol, but in Britain the Teddy Boys embodied the rebellious spirit with their enormous quiffs, sculpted with the aid of Brylcreem.

New innovations in the fifties included the Wimpy Bar in 1955 and Premium Bonds in 1956. There was a craze for yo-yos, 3D spectacles, I Spy books and Hula-Hoops in the late 1950s. Car ownership more than doubled in the decade, despite the Suez crisis of 1956 and the ensuing petrol shortage. This did not deter Harold Macmillan from saying in his 1957 election campaign that Britain had 'never had it so good'. Some felt otherwise, and the first campaign for nuclear disarmament (CND) took place in 1958.

Events

In 1951 the Festival of Britain was a 'tonic to the nation', and even though the much-loved King George VI died unexpectedly the following year, people felt that a new era was dawning. Queen Elizabeth II's coronation in 1953 seemed to mark the end of the years of austerity.

With over a million television sets in use by 1951, the BBC brought the main sporting events into the home, making commentators such as Kenneth Wolstenholme household names. Stanley Matthews won his first FA Cup medal in 1953, when Blackpool beat Bolton Wanderers 4–3. In the same year Len Hutton and Denis Compton (see p. 130) helped to reclaim the Ashes from Australia at the Oval. The BBC's *Sportsview*, introduced by Peter Dimmock, began in 1955, but was replaced by *Grandstand* in 1958. Between 1955 and 1959 Donald Campbell set a series of world water-speed records in *Bluebird K7*, progressing from 202mph to 260mph. The first Briton to win the world motor-racing championship was Mike Hawthorn, in 1958.

◁△▽ On 4 May 1951 the Festival of Britain opened. A derelict 27-acre site had been transformed into an exhibition 'to show our pride in Britain's past, our confidence in her future'. This event, which marked the centenary of the Great Exhibition of 1851, was described by Herbert Morrison as 'the people giving themselves a pat on the back'. The Dome of Discovery and the Skylon were the two great landmarks, but only the Festival Hall survived after the exhibition. By the time it closed in September, 8.5 million visits had been made. Abram Games designed the logo which adorned the posters and literature. The fun fair at Battersea boasted Rowland Emett's cartoon-style railway and the Guinness Clock, where animated zoo animals whirled around every hour.

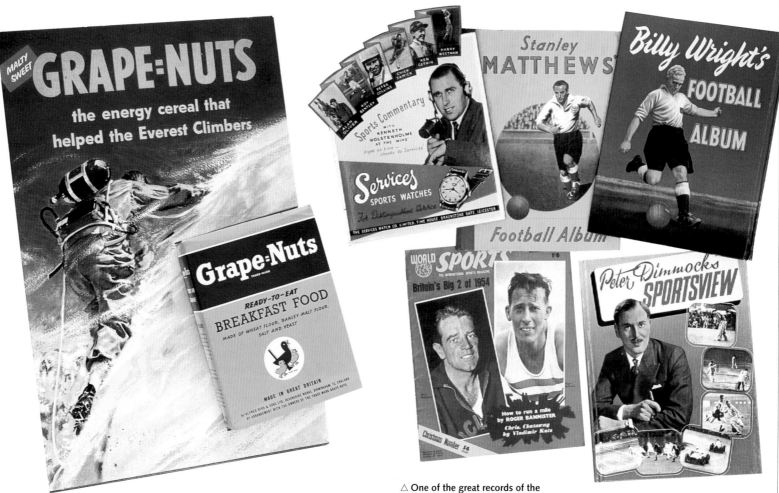

△ In 1953 the forbidding summit of Mount Everest was reached for the first time, by Edmund Hillary and Sherpa Tenzing, his Nepalese guide. An advertising campaign inspired by the conquest was launched by the makers of Grape Nuts, created in America in 1897 to benefit 'brain and nerve centres'.

△ One of the great records of the running track was established in 1954, when Roger Bannister ran the mile in under four minutes. He was supported in his attempt by fellow graduates Chris Chataway and Chris Brasher.

▽ Anticipation of the coronation on 2 June 1953 was heightened as the shops filled with souvenirs. Wrappers for sweets and bread marked the event, and Welgar Shredded Wheat offered a cut-out coronation coach. A Hovis periscope was an advantage in a crowd.

House and home

Many young couples setting up home in the 1950s embraced the new, bold fabric patterns, furniture that displayed unmistakably contemporary lines, and the bright colours, often accompanied by geometric designs, that were appearing on crockery. Housewives now wanted to colour co-ordinate their rooms, so fridges, washing machines, toilet soaps and toilet paper could all be bought in a variety of colours. A growing emphasis on hygiene encouraged the use of light plastics for household goods, while the easily cleaned Formica was ideal for kitchen surfaces and furniture. Such innovations made for a more leisurely domestic life.

sputnik jam dish

It's so easy *& cheap too!* to be bright and clean with
LANCASTER CLOTH
on your TABLES and SHELVES

Made by JAS. WILLIAMSON & SON LTD. LANCASTER

△ Plastic was welcomed as a hygienic material, whether in the form of a handy clothes brush posing as a duck or a sputnik-shaped jam dish. The automatic teamaker was seen as the ultimate in luxury living.

△ Without servants, the housewife was responsible for the cleanliness and look of her kitchen. It was a role in which she was encouraged to take great pride.

▽ The passion for do-it-yourself grew throughout the decade, and 1955 saw the arrival of *Practical Householder*, which showed how to build a sink unit or cupboards, and the best way to unblock a drain. Wives proved that they could join in, but power tools like the Black & Decker or Wolf electric drill were for the man. Following Polycell wallpaper paste (1954), came Polyfilla, a useful new DIY product launched in 1956.

Newnes DO-IT-YOURSELF Magazine
The PRACTICAL HOUSEHOLDER
OCTOBER 1957 1'3
Editor: F.J.CAMM

Wolf Cub
PLASTIC Toy Drill Set
A CLOCKWORK COMPLETE
Made in England
SCALE MODEL BELT SANDER

Peter Pan REGD. **Wolf Cub** Plastic Toy Drill Set
"Now I can copy my Dad"

17'6
Wonderwork Standard
Paint ROLLER
Makes Home Decorating Quicker-Cleaner-Easier

cleaner easier smoother

NEW DISCOVERY
POLYFILLA
THE CELLULOSE FILLER WITH THE AMAZING POSITIVE BOND for Plaster, Brick and Wood, etc.

EVERI
POLYSTYRENE WALL

△ The new idea in furnishing was the modular system called G-Plan (from 1953): 'you assemble, piece by piece, your own individual room arrangements – they harmonise perfectly.'

▽ 'Brilliant gay colours make brighter work of household chores.'

▷ Formica had been invented in America in 1913, and started to be used to laminate furniture during the 1920s. Sales took off in the 1950s as the new colours caught the mood of the moment. Raymond Loewy created a range of decorative patterns in 1957, but the wood-grain effects continued to be popular.

Isn't life COLOURFUL...

with clean-at-a-wipe

FORMICA!

125

Products

After years of rationing, the early 1950s saw the period of privation draw to a welcome close. Restrictions on soap, paper and petrol ceased in 1950, and the sweet ration was ended in time for the coronation of Queen Elizabeth in 1953. All rationing came to an end in 1954. The lifting of restrictions on paper encouraged publishers of magazines and comics to increase their size and bring out many new titles, notably the *Eagle* comic in 1950.

Some chocolate bars anticipated the end of rationing, such as Fry's Punch, which contained the three most popular tastes – chocolate, caramel and fudge. Bounty went on limited trial in 1951, and in 1955 was being advertised as 'new … far and away the most exotic chocolate treat'. Other new arrivals were Wagon Wheels (1954), Week-End (1957), Picnic and Galaxy (both 1958), and Opal Fruits and Munchies (both 1959).

△ The new trend was for filter-tipped cigarettes like Bachelor (1950). Using less tobacco, they were slightly cheaper, but their popularity also derived from the vague awareness that filters were better for health. King-size brands like Kingsway (1959) appeared towards the end of the 1950s, although the five-inch length of the novelty brand Joy Stick was just for fun.

You can taste the Fruit!

ROWNTREE'S FRUIT GUMS

▽ A few confectionery lines were launched before rationing ended. Rowntree's Polo and Mars' Spangles had both come on the market in 1948. Barker & Dobson responded to the growing appeal of television with their selection, a handy assortment to pass around.

△ A profusion of money-off coupons dropped through the letter-box to boost sales of new beauty soaps like Breeze, Astral and Camay (1958), and washing-up liquids like Lux and Quix.

▽ During the 1950s a new range of synthetic organic detergents came to the aid of washday. Fab had arrived in 1949, followed by Tide (1950), Surf (1952), Daz (1953), Omo (1954) and Fairy Snow (1957). Persil ran a publicity campaign that ensured mothers worried about the whiteness of their wash: 'Someone's Mum doesn't know what someone's Mum ought to know. That Persil washes whiter.' Biological detergents were added in the 1960s.

Self-service

During the early 1950s a few shops converted to self-service. It was a new experience for shoppers: 'Pay as you go out. The assistant puts what you have bought into your own basket and gives you a receipt.' A new approach to packaging design was needed. It was now essential that packs caught the eye of the shopper with brighter colours and bolder designs.

Later in the decade supermarkets were first introduced. This revolution in shopping was accompanied by a new, aggressive style of marketing, already familiar in America. The lure of money-off coupons, on-pack promotions, 'flash' packs and price reductions was reinforced by television commercials. At this time the market for breakfast cereals was expanding rapidly. The new excitement was sugar-coated brands like Kellogg's Frosted Flakes (Tony the Tiger appeared in 1955) and Quaker's Sugar Puffs, both of which were launched in 1954. Sugar Ricicles came in 1955, supported by the children's favourite Noddy. Other new cereals included Shreddies in 1953 and Cubs in 1958. Finally, in 1954, a new confection rolled out; each Wagon Wheel came in its own yellow and red pack.

◁ As a range of new drinks aimed at women appeared on the market, the actress Diana Dors found a Godwin particularly irresistible.

▽ Many breakfast cereals were produced and packaged to appeal to children. Sugar-coated varieties appeared in boxes that depicted characters they loved and there were often masks or models to cut out.

△ The self-service basket of the 1950s was filled with innovative products. Popular among frozen foods were Bird's Eye fish fingers (1955). The chocolate drink Nesquik came in the same year.

Maxwell House instant coffee (1954), along with Nescafé (1939), increased awareness of this convenient new beverage. Kraft Dairylea cheese spread came in 1951 and Tetley's tea bags in 1952. Washing-up liquids like Quix (1948) and Squezy (1956) tackled greasy plates, while Flash cleaned up from 1958. Tate & Lyle's Mr Cube fought off nationalisation of the sugar industry (1949–52). The market for soft toilet tissue was growing: Andrex gave away thousands of tiny rolls (see above) around the mid-1950s.

MAKES COOKING SO EASY

△ During the 1950s a growing number of men became familiar with the kitchen, helping with the washing up and the easier aspects of cooking.

△ The Bourn-vita mug, with its nightcap, was a favourite nocturnal companion.

▷ The preparation of meals was made much easier by devices such as the pressure cooker and the food mixer. Most often a Sunbeam or Kenwood Chef, the latter was supplied with a range of attachments for tasks such as mincing meat, liquidizing, extracting juice and grinding coffee.

It's so easy to cook with.... Prestige

Fashion

A new world of fabrics and styles opened up for the fashion-conscious. For many women in the early 1950s, the preferred casual look was tight shirt-style tops that accentuated generous skirts. Pencil-line skirts and close-fitting suits were popular town wear. Man-made fibres ensured that pleats were permanent, and blouses and shirts made of Polyester, for example, were drip-dry and 'minimum-iron'. Among the other new artificial fabrics were Crimplene, Acrilan, Courtelle and Dacron. Women's shoes ranged from the 3¼-inch stiletto to the leather or suede bootee. Mail-order catalogues flourished – hire purchase was becoming increasingly common – and they reflected the blossoming of teenage styles.

Fashions for young men focused on the working-class teenager. The predominant look was the Teddy boy's defiant long, velvet-collared jacket, 'bootlace' tie, 'drainpipe' trousers and crepe-soled 'brothel creepers' (the alternative was the 'winkle picker', with its long, pointed toe) – all capped by greased-back, quiffed hair.

A MURGATROYD Product

Will-o'-the-Wisp
BY MINSTER

FULLY FASHIONED NYLONS

△ The bikini was the latest fashion in swimwear, but synthetic materials achieved some striking effects with the one-piece costume.

▷ A Morphy-Richards electric hair dryer in trendy blue plastic for mum, and a toy electric iron for daughter.

◁ Nylon had been marketed in America during the 1940s. in the 1950s ultra-sheer nylon stockings, cheaper and longer-lasting than silk, proved to be a fast seller.

▷ Brylcreem was launched in 1928 by the County Chemical Company, for use by hairdressers. When it went on general sale in the 1930s, it was linked to athletic prowess. During the war RAF pilots were nicknamed the 'Brylcreem Boys'. The cricketer Denis Compton, who also played football for Arsenal, promoted the product in the early 1950s.

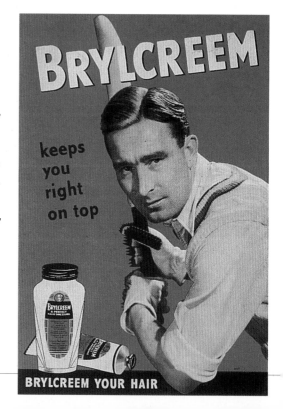

BRYLCREEM

keeps you right on top

BRYLCREEM YOUR HAIR

△ New liquid shampoos and home perms were introduced to cater for the flowing hair styles seen in the movies, where British stars were now making their mark. The Pin-Up showcard shows Hy Hazell, Sally Howes, Dinah Sheridan and Jane Hylton.

▽ *John Bull* magazine's covers captured typical scenes of the 1950s such as the appeal of a sunny holiday or the trials of choosing a fabric design. Laundrettes opened up a new social scene; the first had appeared in London in 1949 and ten years later there were some 2000 throughout the country.

△ Max Factor set up a theatrical shop in LA in 1908, and later sold make-up to film studios. By the 1950s everyone could buy his Hollywood glamour.

Travel and holidays

In 1951 the weekend paper *Reveille* reported that more people were looking for new ways to find a cheap holiday, such as camping, caravanning or working on farms – 110,000 people spent time there under a holidays-on-the-land scheme.

Things were better by 1955 when most workers were entitled to two weeks' paid holiday. There were now over three million cars on Britain's roads, but as a result of the Suez crisis of 1956, petrol was in short supply. This boosted sales of small cars, among them the Volkswagen Beetle. In 1959 came the revolutionary Mini; designed by Alec Issigonis and produced by Morris, it combined convenience, fuel economy and style.

◁ The remote-control Driving Test (operated by a magnet) was a realistic game of skill in which a car was driven around the streets and then parked.

△ The Italian firm Piaggio began to make the Vespa scooter in 1946, and by 1951 it was being produced under licence in Bristol. Over a million Vespas were on Europe's roads by 1955. Lambretta scooters, made by Innocenti of Milan, were launched c. 1947.

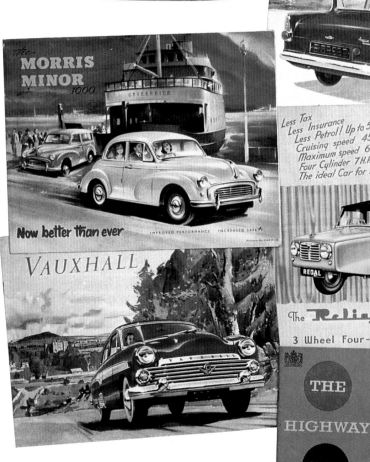

◁ The American-influenced bulbous car bodies of the early 1950s were replaced by new designs like that of 1957's Vauxhall Victor (which was criticized for its American style) and the Ford Anglia of 1959, with its reverse-slope rear window.

ARIEL
The Modern Motorcycle
1958

◁ The top-of-the-range Ariel – 1000cc, four-cylinder, with twin crankshafts, built-in illuminated instrument panel and pillion foot rests – was guaranteed to impress the discerning young lady. It sold for £270 plus £66 purchase tax.

▽ More choice for more people: a trip to the coast, a holiday camp or the adventure of foreign travel with the added attraction of new cuisine. Travel to the Continent was cheaper by coach but quicker by plane.

PORTSMOUTH & SOUTHSEA

Blackpool
FOR HAPPY HEALTHY HOLIDAYS

Why travelling **GLOBAL** is a Grand experience...

LUNN'S

KING-FLIGHT HOLIDAYS 1959

Butlin's where you make new friends!

FREE BROCHURE

holidays in **ITALY** 1955

BARTEX sunglasses

Sun Flight HOLIDAYS

TRAVEL

1957

THOS. COOK & SON LTD   DEAN & DAWSON LTD

▽ With the introduction of the De Havilland Comet 1 on 2 May 1952, BOAC inaugurated the first scheduled passenger service by jet airliner, almost halving the previous flight time. But in 1954 two Comets crashed and they were withdrawn until 1958, when the Comet 4 offered the first jet service between London and New York.

passengers and freight at London Airport. The cover design of ... pression of a Comet III which is in production, but will not be ... about 1956. The Comet III, which is 111 feet long from nose to tail, ... than the Comet II, and can also ... lle fuel tanks. In both ... is 115 feet.

Popular music

The arrival of rock'n'roll coincided with the success of television shows based around popular music. Bill Haley and His Comets had started to rock in 1955, and Elvis Presley entered the British charts in 1956 with *Heartbreak Hotel*, *Blue Suede Shoes*, *Hound Dog* and *Love Me Tender*. The BBC's *Six-Five Special* hosted by Pete Murray added fuel to the fervour in 1957, as Bill Haley toured Britain. ITV's answer was the show *Oh Boy!*.

Top Ten charts had begun in 1955, highlighting the popularity of the new music. Teenagers listened gathered around the Dansette record player (opposite) or the jukebox in coffee bars. Serious discussion could be heard on BBC TV's *Juke Box Jury*, chaired by David Jacobs from 1959. Hits were now coming from British stars like Tommy Steele, Cliff Richard, Billy Fury and Adam Faith.

▷ Lonnie Donegan was the King of Skiffle. His most memorable song was *Rock Island Line* (1955).

▽ Bill Haley and His Comets' record *Rock around the Clock* shot to the top in Britain during 1955. The following year the film of the same name was released and then *Don't Knock the Rock* (the girl in a swimsuit was considered indecent and was covered over at the time).

△ Popular music in the early 1950s was a mix of styles – Ted Heath's Band, skiffle, traditional jazz, crooners like Frank Sinatra, the piano of Winifred Atwell and Russ Conway, and the voices of Doris Day, Alma Cogan, Frankie Vaughan, Max Bygraves, Perry Como and Pat Boone.

△ Elvis Presley, having rocked the music world, went on to conquer Hollywood. Beginning in the mid-1950s, he made a string of 33 films, including *Love Me Tender* (1956), *Jailhouse Rock* and *Loving You* (both 1957), and, following his stint in the army, *G.I. Blues* (1960).

◁ The Platters made their mark in Britain in 1956 with *The Great Pretender*. Cliff Richard's *Move It* (1958) was the first home-grown rock'n'roll hit. The following year the singer scored his first number one with *Living Doll* and followed up with *Travellin' Light*.

Film

Movie-goers wanted new experiences. Capturing the rebel spirit were the leather-clad Marlon Brando in *The Wild One* (1953) and James Dean in *East of Eden* (1954). Both went on quickly to make a further film, Brando *On the Waterfront* (1954) and Dean *Rebel Without a Cause* (1955). Other films shocked with their sexual explicitness – *From Here to Eternity* (1953) with Burt Lancaster and Deborah Kerr had a famous romp on the beach, while *Peyton Place* (1957) revealed the scandals of life in a small town.

In science fiction *Forbidden Planet* (1956) made its mark, while Alfred Hitchcock produced some of his finest work in *Dial M for Murder* with Grace Kelly (see right) and *Rear Window* (both 1954), *Vertigo* (1958) and the horrific *Psycho* (1960). Nevertheless, the screens were still full of beautiful pouting women – Jayne Mansfield, Diana Dors, Zsa Zsa Gabor, Sabrina, Joan Collins, Brigitte Bardot, Jane Russell, Elizabeth Taylor and Marilyn Monroe, who starred in classics such as *The Seven Year Itch* (1955) and *Some Like it Hot* (1959).

▽ **Alec Guinness starred as** *The Man in the White Suit* **(1951) and took other character roles in** *The Ladykillers* **(1955) and** *The Bridge on the River Kwai* **(1957), for which he won an Oscar.**

△▷ Film magazines took fans into a world peopled by stars like David Niven and Shirley MacLaine (above right in *Around the World in Eighty Days*, 1956) and the comic Norman Wisdom in *One Good Turn* (above, 1954).

Ealing Studios present another comedy:

**ALEC GUINNESS
JOAN GREENWOOD
CECIL PARKER** in

THE MAN IN THE WHITE SUIT

A MICHAEL BALCON PRODUCTION

DIRECTED BY ALEXANDER MACKENDRICK

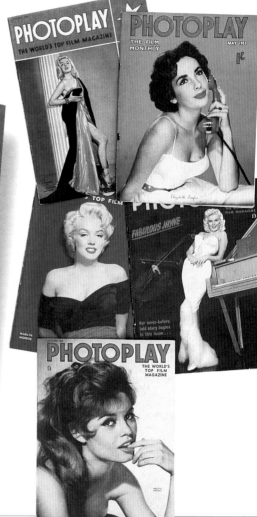

The men who broke the bank — and lost the cargo!

EALING STUDIOS present

Alec Guinness & Stanley Holloway
with Sidney James & Alfie Bass

as THE LAVENDER HILL MOB

Directed by CHARLES CRICHTON

A MICHAEL BALCON PRODUCTION
Original screenplay by T.E.B. CLARKE

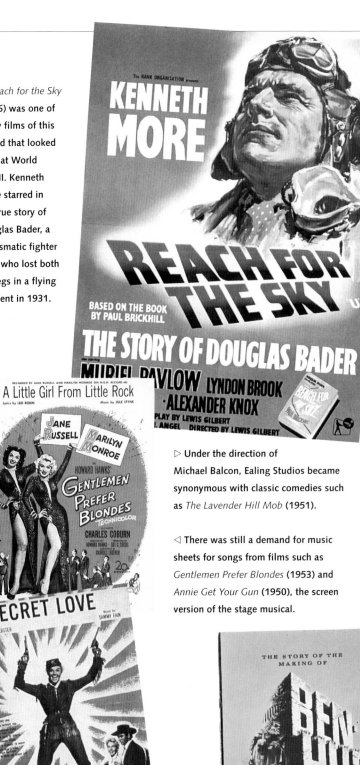

The RANK ORGANISATION presents

KENNETH MORE

REACH FOR THE SKY

BASED ON THE BOOK
BY PAUL BRICKHILL

THE STORY OF DOUGLAS BADER

also starring MURIEL PAVLOW LYNDON BROOK ALEXANDER KNOX

SCREENPLAY BY LEWIS GILBERT
PRODUCED BY DANIEL M. ANGEL DIRECTED BY LEWIS GILBERT

▷ *Reach for the Sky* (1956) was one of many films of this period that looked back at World War II. Kenneth More starred in the true story of Douglas Bader, a charismatic fighter pilot who lost both his legs in a flying accident in 1931.

▷ Under the direction of Michael Balcon, Ealing Studios became synonymous with classic comedies such as *The Lavender Hill Mob* (1951).

◁ There was still a demand for music sheets for songs from films such as *Gentlemen Prefer Blondes* (1953) and *Annie Get Your Gun* (1950), the screen version of the stage musical.

THE STORY OF THE MAKING OF

BEN-HUR

A TALE OF THE CHRIST

FROM METRO-GOLDWYN-MAYER

EL CID

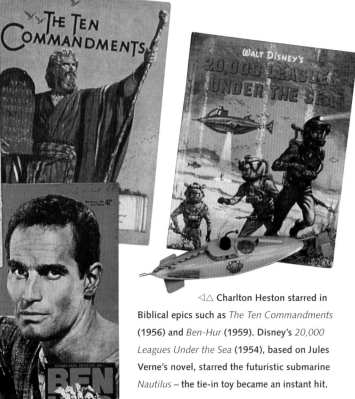

THE TEN COMMANDMENTS

WALT DISNEY'S 20,000 LEAGUES UNDER THE SEA

BEN HUR

◁△ Charlton Heston starred in Biblical epics such as *The Ten Commandments* (1956) and *Ben-Hur* (1959). Disney's *20,000 Leagues Under the Sea* (1954), based on Jules Verne's novel, starred the futuristic submarine *Nautilus* – the tie-in toy became an instant hit.

Radio and television

The listening public had grown greatly attached to the radio in the 1940s, and many programmes became national institutions. When *Housewives' Choice* came on, women all over Britain would sit down to listen with a cup of tea. Other programmes were to be just as popular – *Woman's Hour* celebrated its thousandth edition in 1950. The following year *The Archers* arrived. Adventure was provided by *P.C. 49* and comedy by *The Navy Lark*, *Round the Horne* and *The Goon Show*.

But it was television that eventually pulled the crowds. The comings and goings of the Grove family were followed on Friday evenings from 1954. Peggy Mount and David Kossoff were the stars of *The Larkins* (1958–64). Magic came from David Nixon and Tommy Cooper, who was also a comic, while Benny Hill's humour caught the mood of the times. *Tonight* with Cliff Michelmore and *Panorama* with Richard Dimbleby debated topical issues. David Attenborough's *Zoo Quest* and Philip Harben's and Fanny Craddock's cookery shows pointed to the future of television.

▽ Smaller, portable radios came on the market in the 1950s. The Bakelite KB model of 1950 was known as the 'toaster' because of its looks and the fact that it produced a lot of heat. An exciting development in the latter years of the decade was the transistor radio – its lack of valves allowed it to be compact.

△ Manufacturers cashed in on the ever-increasing popularity of the new medium. Among the novelties they produced were TV savings banks, TV jigsaws, TV cigarette dispensers and, for the real couch potato, the Tea-V-Tray with a ready supply of TV snacks.

▽ A crucial part of television viewing was ensuring the best reception, and the suburban skyline was now dominated by H-shaped television aerials. Cars caused interference, so motorists were advised to fit suppressors to the ignition.

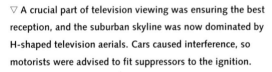

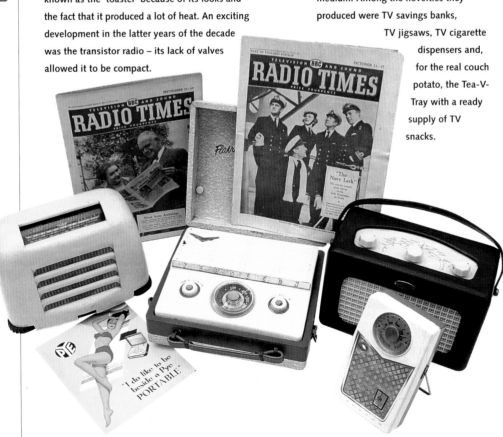

So many end up with BUSH

△ Eamonn Andrews was the consummate host of the children's show *Crackerjack* (1955). Quiz shows were much in demand: *Take Your Pick* with Michael Miles, *Double Your Money* with Hughie Green and, from 1958, *Beat the Clock* with Bruce Forsyth. Jack Warner starred in *Dixon of Dock Green* and Richard Greene in *The Adventures of Robin Hood*. American humour arrived in the shape of Bilko in *The Phil Silvers Show* (1957–60); British favourites were *Hancock's Half Hour* (1956–60) and Jimmy Edwards in *Whack-O!* (1956–60 and 1971) and *The Army Game* (1957–61).

Space

There has always been a fascination with space travel. H. G. Wells caught the popular imagination with books like *The Time Machine* (1895) and *The First Men in the Moon* (1901). Buck Rogers came to life in the 25th century in the American comic strips of 1929. Flash Gordon first appeared in America in 1934. Both heroes came to British magazines in the late 1930s, in *Everybody's Weekly* and *Modern World*, respectively.

Superman was another American creation, a comic-book hero from 1938. Batman appeared the following year. For Britons, it was Dan Dare in the *Eagle* (1950) who, with his companion Digby, struck out into space to take on the Mekon in the story 'Marooned on Mercury'. *Eagle*'s sister comic, *Girl*, followed in 1951, but the adventures of the airline pilot Kitty Hawke and her all-girl crew were soon replaced by the nursing story 'Susan of St. Bride's'.

1950s

◁ The *Eagle* was launched in April 1950, priced 3d. It was the creation of the Reverend Marcus Morris, who wanted to provide boys with better reading material than crime comics imported from America. On the cover each week were the adventures of Dan Dare, Pilot of the Future, drawn by Frank Hampson. The *Eagle* survived until 1969.

△▽ Sci-fi stories, with their explosive picture covers, opened up a new world for many youngsters. Walking robots arrived from Japan, while in 1952 *Lion* appeared, featuring Captain Condor, a space pilot from the year 3000 who was banished to an uncharted moon called Zor.

△ There was a great demand among fans of Dan Dare for toys and games that captured the excitement of his supersonic adventures – cosmic-ray-guns, walkie-talkie sets with push-button planetary selectors, rocket guns with a secret message chamber and the high-frequency resonator with its spectroscopic beam converter.

Toys

After the lean post-war years the toy industry bounced back with growing confidence. Many businesses were set up soon after the war by ex-servicemen such as Leslie Smith and Rodney Smith (unrelated) who, having left the Royal Navy, established a small die-cast business in London. A former Army engineer, Jack Odell, joined the Smiths, who founded Lesney Products. The breakthrough came in 1953 when the firm made over a million scale models of the Queen's coronation coach. The highly successful Matchbox Series of models followed.

Comics were another area of the children's market to undergo a transformation. After the end of paper shortages in 1950, new titles appeared fast, the *Eagle* that same year. Free gifts reappeared in 1954 – particularly coveted was the space gun given away with the first issue of *Tiger*, which featured Roy of the Rovers. Meanwhile Dennis the Menace had been causing havoc since joining the *Beano* in 1951.

▷▽ An assortment of toys that became favourites in the 1950s. Some – for example Bayko and Minibrix – had been around in the 1930s; others, like Cluedo and Subbuteo, had been launched in the post-war years. In 1954 Scrabble arrived in Britain from America, where it had been a great hit the previous year. The hula-hoop craze swept the world in 1958 and inevitably toy manufacturers made hula dolls like the clockwork Spin-A-Hoop. Mobo toys, made in England by D. Sabel & Co, were for small children.

△ Dinky toys were the leading die-cast models, but in 1956 Mettoy, who had been producing toys since 1933, created the Corgi range of scale models, which boasted plastic windows and greater attention to detail. By 1959 the firm had introduced 'glideamatic suspension', which made Corgi vehicles run more smoothly. Lesney's Matchbox Series of miniature vehicles appeared in 1953, priced at 1s 6d each.

▽ In 1952 Airfix launched the Golden Hind plastic kit in a bag, selling at 2s through Woolworths, to compete with American kits like Merit and Revell.

△ A wide choice of comics for boys and girls: *School Friend* (1950), *Girl* (1951), *Topper* (1953), *T.V. Fun* (1953), *Tiger* (1954), *Beezer* (1956) and *Bunty* (1958).

▷ Rosebud dolls, which arrived in 1947, were made from various materials until the late 1950s, when a malleable plastic allowed the hair to be rooted.

143

Playtime

Children's television relied heavily on puppets, and the late 1940s and 1950s saw a string of such characters. Muffin the Mule had been around since 1946 and was joined by his friend Peregrine the penguin; Mr Turnip appeared with the comedian Humphrey Lestocq on the programme *Whirligig*, along with the cowboy Hank and his horse Silver King. The twin pigs Pinky and Perky, with their comic voices, came in 1957.

Sooty first appeared on television in 1952, although his creator, Harry Corbett, had used a nameless hand-puppet bear in his conjuring act since 1948. Terry Hall introduced Lenny the Lion in 1956, while another ventriloquist was Peter Brough with Archie Andrews, whose radio show, *Educating Archie* (1950–60), moved to ITV in 1958 and continued until 1959. Richard Hearne provided children's comedy with his character Mr Pastry from 1950. The Noddy books were written by Enid Blyton; the first of these, *Little Noddy Goes to Toyland*, had appeared at the end of 1949.

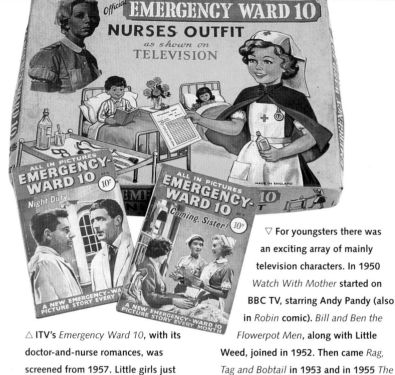

△ ITV's *Emergency Ward 10*, with its doctor-and-nurse romances, was screened from 1957. Little girls just wanted the nurse's outfit.

▽ For youngsters there was an exciting array of mainly television characters. In 1950 *Watch With Mother* started on BBC TV, starring Andy Pandy (also in *Robin* comic). *Bill and Ben the Flowerpot Men*, along with Little Weed, joined in 1952. Then came *Rag, Tag and Bobtail* in 1953 and in 1955 *The Woodentops* (see p. 120), starring Spotty the dog with his weird bark and silly walk.

▷ *The Lone Ranger*, **starring Clayton Moore**, started on television in 1956. Perhaps the best known of the fictional TV cowboys, the Lone Ranger appeared, mounted on his rearing horse Silver, on packets of Puffed Wheat in 1958; each box contained a free black mask.

△ Throughout the 1950s, cowboys (and sometimes Indians) were part of every boy's playtime – in books, badges, games, guns, films and TV programmes. Disney's *Davy Crockett* was screened in 1955 and the Cisco Kid, on his horse Diablo, hit town in 1954. Even the horses were famous – Champion the Wonder Horse was ridden by Gene Autry, while Trigger was Roy Rogers' mount. *Rawhide*, with Clint Eastwood, first went on the air in the USA in 1959.

The 1960s

Known retrospectively as the Swinging Sixties, the decade became associated with a concoction of many things that brought Britain to the forefront: the birth of British pop music and fashion; winning the World Cup in 1966; technological achievements such as the Hawker Harrier, the world's first vertical take-off plane (1966) and Concorde (1969).

This was the permissive decade. *Lady Chatterley's Lover* was published in 1960 after winning a famous obscenity trial.

Challenges to authority were made in the pages of *Private Eye*, *Oz* and *IT*, while the BBC's *That Was The Week That Was* with David Frost and Lance Percival pushed television satire to its limits. In the theatre the rock musical *Hair* (1968) included a celebrated nude scene, paving the way for the all-nude review *Oh! Calcutta!* two years later. The contraceptive pill became available on prescription from 1963, heralding a new reproductive freedom for women.

Most people had televisions by the end of the decade. *Coronation Street* first aired in 1960. Live trans-Atlantic television was made possible by Telstar, the satellite launched in 1962. BBC 2 went on the air in 1964 and was the first channel to have colour (1967). Gerry Anderson's magic brought us the sci-fi puppets in *Captain Scarlet* and *Thunderbirds*, while the relative realism of *Dr Who and the Daleks* scared many a small viewer.

People began to do the twist in 1961, and the Bossa Nova soon followed. But it was the music and songs of the Beatles, Rolling Stones, Kinks, Dusty Springfield and many more that really set the pace of the sixties. Youth culture took the lead. Jean Shrimpton and Twiggy modelled the latest short dresses by Mary Quant and the innovative hairstyles of Vidal Sassoon. Boutiques and discotheques were the chic places to go. By the end of the decade Flower Power became the message, manifesting itself in everything from psychedelic fabrics to peaceful rebellion and experimentation with hallucinogenic drugs.

Memorable headlines announced the death of Winston Churchill (1965), the Great Train Robbery (1963), and the moon landing – the technical achievement of the century. But the greatest shock was the assassination of President Kennedy in 1963.

Events

During the 1960s scandal, sport and space dominated the headlines. The Profumo affair of 1963 shook Britain and the Macmillan government, causing the Secretary of State for War to resign. In sport Britain had four world champions in Formula One racing: Jim Clark, Graham Hill, John Surtees and Jackie Stewart. In 1966 England's football team won the World Cup, and the following year Francis Chichester, at 65, sailed alone around the world in his yacht *Gipsy Moth IV*. In 1969 Britain's Ann Jones won Wimbledon and Tony Jacklin was British Open golf champion.

The space race brought a string of achievements. At first the Russians took the initiative with their *Sputnik* satellite of 1957 and in 1961, sent the first man into space; the USA's Alan Shepard went up three weeks later. John Glenn and then Scott Carpenter orbited the earth in 1962. A Russian cosmonaut and then an American made the first space walks in 1965. After more missions, lunar orbits and unmanned landings, in 1969 the Americans Neil Armstrong and Buzz Aldrin were the first men to walk on the moon.

▽ The first man in space was the Soviet cosmonaut Yuri Gagarin, who in April 1961 made an orbit of the earth in his spaceship *Vostok*. The American astronaut Neil Armstrong, commander of *Apollo 11*, set foot on the moon on 20 July 1969: 'That's one small step for man, one giant leap for mankind.'

△ An affair between John Profumo, Secretary of State for War, and Christine Keeler – who also had liaisons with Russian diplomats – ended in 1961, but the scandal was not revealed until 1963.

▽ Henry Cooper, who was the British and Empire heavyweight champion in 1959, fought Cassius Clay (later Muhammad Ali) in 1963. He lost but was one of the few to floor the American

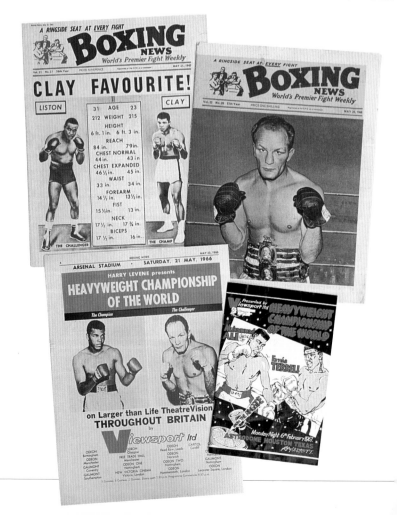

▷ The first football World Cup had been held in 1930 in Uruguay, which won the event. In 1966 England hosted the event, in a climate of football fever generated in part by the much-loved mascot World Cup Willie. The final, between England and Germany, was played at Wembley on 30 July. The Germans took an early lead, but then Geoff Hurst and Martin Peters put England ahead, only for Germany to equalize in the game's dying minutes. During extra time Hurst scored twice – the first goal was controversial – to give Captain Bobby Moore and manager Alf Ramsay a decisive 4–2 victory.

Products

An increasing choice of branded products filled supermarket shelves, among them frozen and chilled items such as ready-made meals, yogurts, and desserts, for most homes now had a refrigerator. Brands were often aimed at children and promoted on TV by popular characters. Breakfast cereals provided an instant meal for hungry kids and busy mums.

Eating an ice cream or lolly in the street was by now more socially acceptable, and in the early 1960s canned soft drinks joined the growing range of convenience products. New brands of cigarettes included B&H Special Filter (1961), Embassy (1962) and Player's No.6 (1965).

△ Since the 1930s sweet cigarettes had been popular with children. But attitudes to smoking were changing in the 1960s and, by the end of the following decade, sweet cigarettes would be 'candy sticks' and the red tips would have disappeared.

▽ Coco Pops were launched in 1961 with Mr Jinks. Sooty's friend Sweep replaced him after the name became Coco Krispies. Cornelius the Cockerel appeared on Corn Flakes packets from 1963, when pop-up toasters were fun.

△ Slimming was a serious pastime. Starch-reduced and calorie-controlled brands kept women trim, along with Eileen Fowler's keep-fit exercises.

New products for the 1960s: Fairy Liquid (1960), J Cloths, Pledge aerosol for 'real wax beauty instantly as you dust', Golden Wonder crisps came in cheese and onion flavour from 1962, Blue Band margarine could now be spread straight from the fridge, Smash (1968) led instant mashed potato brands (the Martians in the TV commericals landed in the early 1970s), Colgate Fluoride arrived in 1964, and the 'ring of confidence' commercial in 1965. Strand cigarettes (1960) failed.

▽ The yogurt revolution took off when real fruit was added. Ski was first with its bilberry flavour in 1963.

▽▷ Ice lollies and choc ices on sticks became a major market during the 1960s, mostly produced by Walls and Lyons Maid. A never-ending supply of 'with it' names were required, among them Fab, Kinky and Zoom. Below: Sugar Smacks (launched 1958) kept pace with each favourite hero.

Fashion

The 1960s made a radical break with the past. London began to swing, 'with it' or 'fab' places being Carnaby Street in the West End and the King's Road, Chelsea. Top models like Jean Shrimpton (early 1960s) and Twiggy (later 1960s) wore the latest fashions, particularly the revealing mini-skirt, and Mary Quant's clothes designs became the byword for chic style. The Biba shop and mail-order business (see p. 178) set the pace in the late 1960s for small boutiques all over the country. Women's hair was shorter, typified by Vidal Sassoon's geometric cut, and eyes were made more appealing with false lashes. Men let their hair grow.

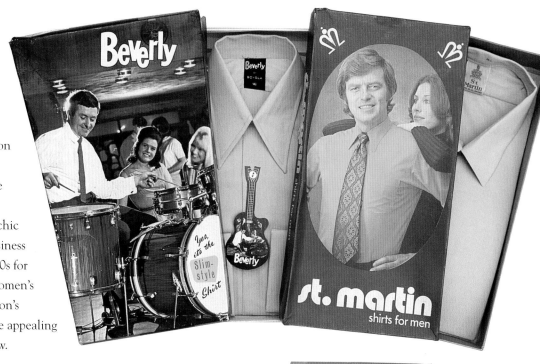

▽ The fresh young looks of Twiggy burst on to the fashion scene in 1966 when the *Daily Express* nominated her 'face of the year'.

△ For generations of men the office shirt had been white. Suddenly the trendy young man could cut a dash with waist-hugging shirts in a wide range of pastel shades.

◁ The elastic roll-on girdle, so popular in the 1950s, now began to lose its appeal. The suspender belt also became redundant with the arrival of elastic-topped stockings such as Pretty Polly Hold-Ups (see p. 146).

△ Magazines like *Honey*, crammed with features on fashion and advertisements for clothes, shoes and cosmetics, appealed to younger women. Baby Doll products, sold by Woolworths, were given a groovy promotional campaign in 1968.

Culture and counterculture

The Establishment was being attacked on all sides during the 1960s. The BBC's satirical programme *That Was The Week That Was* (1962–3), known as *TW3* (see p. 162), broke new ground by making fun of politicians, religion and class. David Frost hosted the show and Millicent Martin sang the theme song. When the 1964 General Election loomed it was taken off the air.

The satirical journal *Punch* was going strong at this time, but it took the more radical *Private Eye* to hit the mark on serious scandals. Launched in 1961, it was edited by Richard Ingrams, and Peter Cook was long a mainstay of the magazine. Richard Neville brought the colourful Australian underground magazine *Oz* to London in 1966.

Another form of counterculture arrived with Mods and Rockers, who made southern seaside resorts a battlefield in 1964. Rockers wore leather jackets and rode motor bikes. More style-conscious, Mods wore sharp lightweight suits or smart jackets over polo necks or Fred Perry shirts and took immense pride in their Italian scooters.

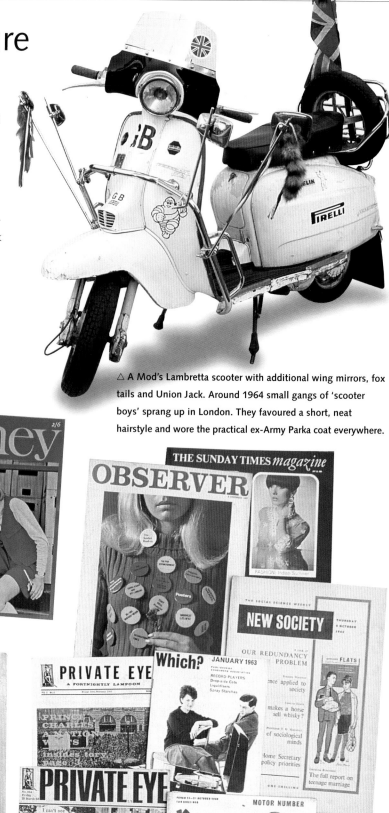

△ A Mod's Lambretta scooter with additional wing mirrors, fox tails and Union Jack. Around 1964 small gangs of 'scooter boys' sprang up in London. They favoured a short, neat hairstyle and wore the practical ex-Army Parka coat everywhere.

△ A clutch of new magazines, including *Which?* (1957), *Private Eye* (1961), *New Society* (1962), *Nova* (1964), *Penthouse* (1969) and the colour supplements of the *Sunday Times* (1962) and *Observer* (1964).

◁△ *Oz* magazine had started in
Australia in 1963 and, almost by chance,
came to London in 1966. Its radical
content of libertarianism, obscenity,
pornography and anti-establishment free
thinking constantly pushed at the limits of
permissiveness. Much of its psychedelically
inspired artwork was done by Martin Sharp.
Tolerance of the magazine ended in 1970
with the 'School Kids' issue, and the
proprietors were prosecuted for obscenity. *Oz*
won, but other underground papers, such as
IT (*International Times*, launched in 1966),
did not survive the costs of litigation.

Leisure

With employment high and most enjoying a reasonable income, the early 1960s saw a growth in consumerism. Leisure time could be enjoyed by shopping, going to the cinema, watching television and travelling abroad. By mid-decade motoring, too, had become a pleasure affordable to 8.5 million car owners.

A considerable number of young people chose to 'drop out' and join the hippy movement that reached its peak during 1967's 'Summer of Love'. This was the era of flower power, transcendental meditation and soft drugs. Procol Harum's *A Whiter Shade of Pale* and the Beatles' *Sergeant Pepper's Lonely Hearts' Club Band* epitomized the music.

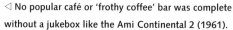

△ The 'sensation of America' came to Britain in 1961 when Chubby Checker's record *Let's Twist Again* stayed in the singles charts for 30 weeks. The Twist became the most popular dance of the decade – now couples danced separately.

▽ As the discotheque scene went wild, handfuls of publicity leaflets were given away in central London – some with stylish topical designs. Westminster City Council banned them in 1970 as they were causing a litter problem.

◁ No popular café or 'frothy coffee' bar was complete without a jukebox like the Ami Continental 2 (1961).

156

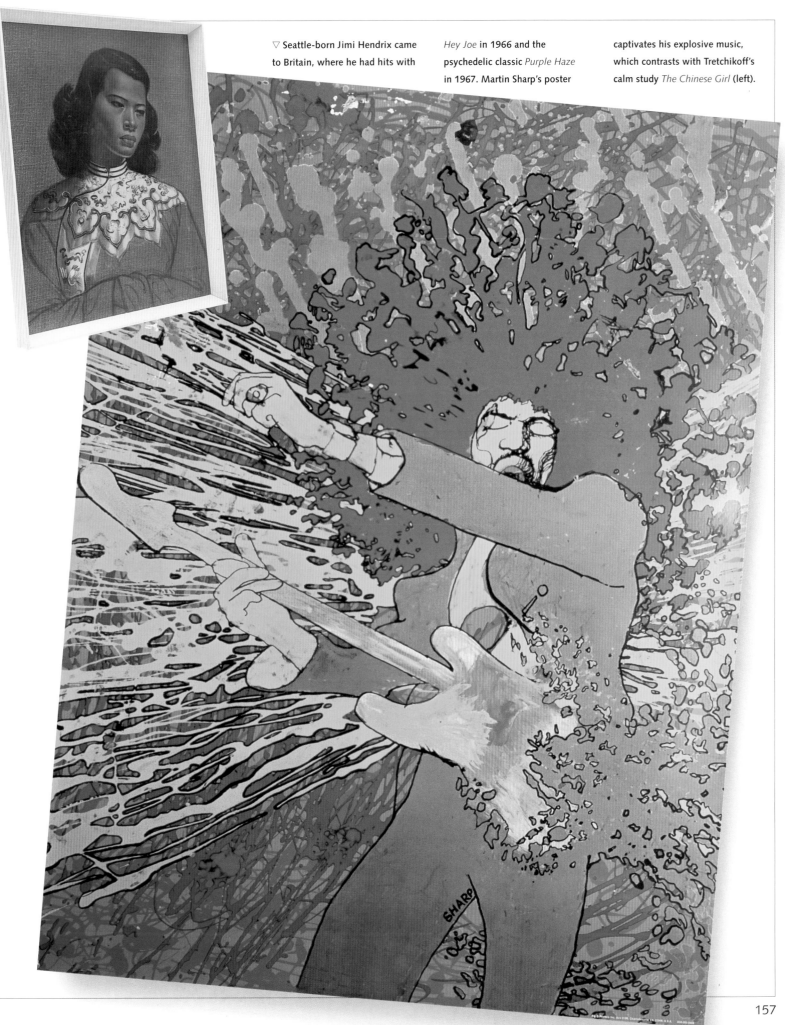

▽ Seattle-born Jimi Hendrix came to Britain, where he had hits with *Hey Joe* in 1966 and the psychedelic classic *Purple Haze* in 1967. Martin Sharp's poster captivates his explosive music, which contrasts with Tretchikoff's calm study *The Chinese Girl* (left).

Pop music

The pop scene of the Swinging Sixties was bursting with vocal groups, solo artists and instrumentalists. But at the outset teenagers had to listen to the latest hits on the café jukebox or a basic record player. Their only other lifeline was a nightly dose of music from Radio Luxembourg or Alan Freeman's *Pick of the Pops* on BBC radio on Sunday afternoon. Then, in 1964, came the offshore pirate stations – Radio Caroline and Radio London – but in 1967 the Government closed them down as a risk to shipping. However, in the reorganization of BBC radio into Radios 1, 2, 3 and 4, Radio 1 became the new station for pop music and ex-pirate radio DJs like Tony Blackburn and John Peel. Television, too, now broadcast pop shows: Cathy McGowan presented ITV's *Ready, Steady, Go*, and from 1964 the BBC had *Top of the Pops*.

◁ Near life-size plastic guitars with Elvis or Beatles insignia inspired many youngsters to follow in their heroes' footsteps.

▽ The Beatles' first chart single, *Love Me Do*, was a Lennon/McCartney song produced by EMI's George Martin; it reached number 17 in 1962. The first of many number ones was *From Me to You* in May 1963. Beatlemania swept America in 1964. The film *A Hard Day's Night* (1964) was followed by *Help!* (1965) and the animated fantasy *Yellow Submarine* in 1968.

△ Britain's home-grown pop idols of the late 1950s and early 1960s were Tommy Steele, Adam Faith, Billy Fury, Marty Wilde and Cliff Richard, whose first number one was *Living Doll* (1959). His films included *The Young Ones* (1961) and *Summer Holiday* (1962).

◁△ An explosion of pop and rock on both sides of the Atlantic included The Everly Brothers' *Cathy's Clown* (1960), Roy Orbison's *Only the Lonely* (1960) and the Surfing Sound of the Beach Boys' *I Get Around* (1964). The Rolling Stones formed in 1962 and from 1964 had a series of hits. Also in that year, the Who arrived and Manfred Mann broke through with *5-4-3-2-1*. The Monkees were brought together in America to make a television series (1966–7). The Bee Gees had hits with *Massachusetts* (1967) and *I've Got to Get a Message to You* (1968). Folk music was led by Joan Baez and the early Bob Dylan. The Eurovision Song Contest gave Sandie Shaw a hit with *Puppet on a String* in 1967; Cliff Richard came second in 1968 with *Congratulations*.

Film

A new wave of British film-making had begun with *Look Back in Anger* (1959), followed by *Saturday Night and Sunday Morning* (1960), *A Taste of Honey* (1961) and *This Sporting Life* (1963). Out of Hollywood came Peter O'Toole as *Lawrence of Arabia* (1962), Elizabeth Taylor as *Cleopatra* (1963), Peter Sellers as *Dr Strangelove* (1964), *Dr Zhivago* (1965), Dustin Hoffman as *The Graduate* and *Bonnie and Clyde* (both 1967), *Butch Cassidy and the Sundance Kid* and *Midnight Cowboy* (both 1969). Clint Eastwood, of TV's *Rawhide*, served up the 'spaghetti western' *A Fistful of Dollars* (1964). New British stars emerged – Julie Christie in *Darling* (1965), Michael Caine in *Alfie* (1966) and Sean Connery as the immortal James Bond.

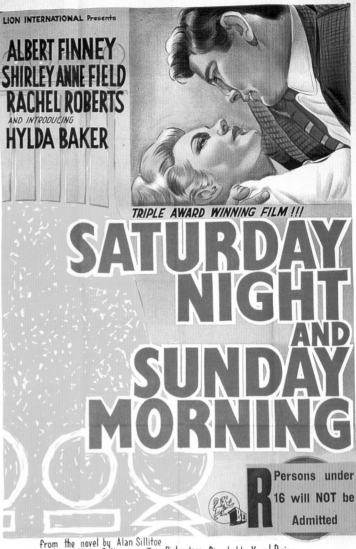

△ *Saturday Night and Sunday Morning* (1960) launched Albert Finney on his film career. Banned briefly for its 'beer-and-sex' content, this raw working-class melodrama transformed British cinema. Another 'social realism' film was *The Loneliness of the Long Distance Runner* (1962) starring Tom Courtenay.

1960s

△▷ The first Bond film was *Dr. No* (1962); this and its successors, notably *From Russia With Love* (1963), *Goldfinger* (1964) and *Thunderball* (1965), made the unknown Sean Connery a movie icon. Ian Fleming's Bond books had been best sellers in the 1950s and 1960s; he also wrote *Chitty Chitty Bang Bang*, which was released as a film in 1968.

△ The space epic *2001: A Space Odyssey* (1968) was directed by Stanley Kubrick, who created sumptuous sets for the Oscar-winning special effects.

▷ There were 28 *Carry On* films, starting in 1958 with *Carry on, Sergeant*. The series caught the British sense of humour, but by the time of *Carry On Camping* (1968) the formula of old jokes and innuendo was rather tired.

▽*The Dirty Dozen* (1967), starring Lee Marvin and Charles Bronson, was one of many Second World War blockbusters released around this time.

▷ The two most popular musicals ever starred Julie Andrews – her Oscar was for the 'supercalifragilisticexpialidocious' *Mary Poppins* (1964) and *The Sound of Music* (1965).

Television

By the end of the 1960s most people in Britain who wanted a TV set had one. This new form of mass entertainment was attracting huge audiences – for example, 18 million regularly watched the twice-weekly kitchen-sink drama *Coronation Street*. *Z Cars* quickly reached 15 million, while *Dr Kildare* (1961–66) attracted roughly the same number of viewers. *The Morecambe and Wise Show* began on ITV in 1961 (the double act had made an unsuccessful series for the BBC in 1954 called *Running Wild*); the show moved to BBC2 in 1968.

The transistor revolution allowed miniaturisation of television and radio sets. Japanese firms like Sony, Hitachi and JVC – whose futuristic Videosphere, below right, dates from around 1966 – were starting to dominate the market. Colour television arrived on BBC2 in 1967 and on BBC1 and ITV two years later.

▷ *Coronation Street* began in December 1960, and quickly established a group of North of England neighbours who were to become national institutions – Ena Sharples (Violet Carson), Elsie Tanner (Pat Phoenix), Ken Barlow (William Roache), Hilda Ogden (Jean Alexander) and Len Fairclough (Peter Adamson).

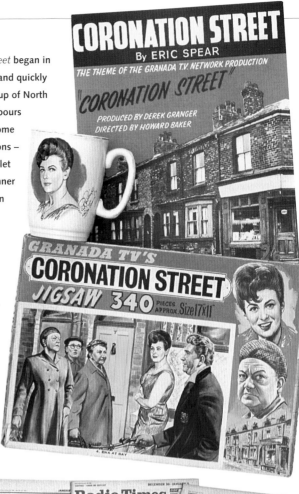

▽ Television drama and comedy included *Harry Worth* (1960–74), *The Likely Lads* (1964–6), *Till Death Us Do Part* (1966–74) with Warren Mitchell as Alf Garnett, Peter Cook and Dudley Moore in *Not Only … But Also* (1965–6 and 1970), *Steptoe and Son* (1962–74) with Wilfred Brambell and Harry H. Corbett, Arthur Lowe in *Dad's Army* (1968–77), *Dr Finlay's Casebook* (from 1962), *Daktari* (1966–9) and *The Forsyte Saga* (1967). From America came the zany *Munsters* (1965–7) and *The Addams Family* (1966–8).

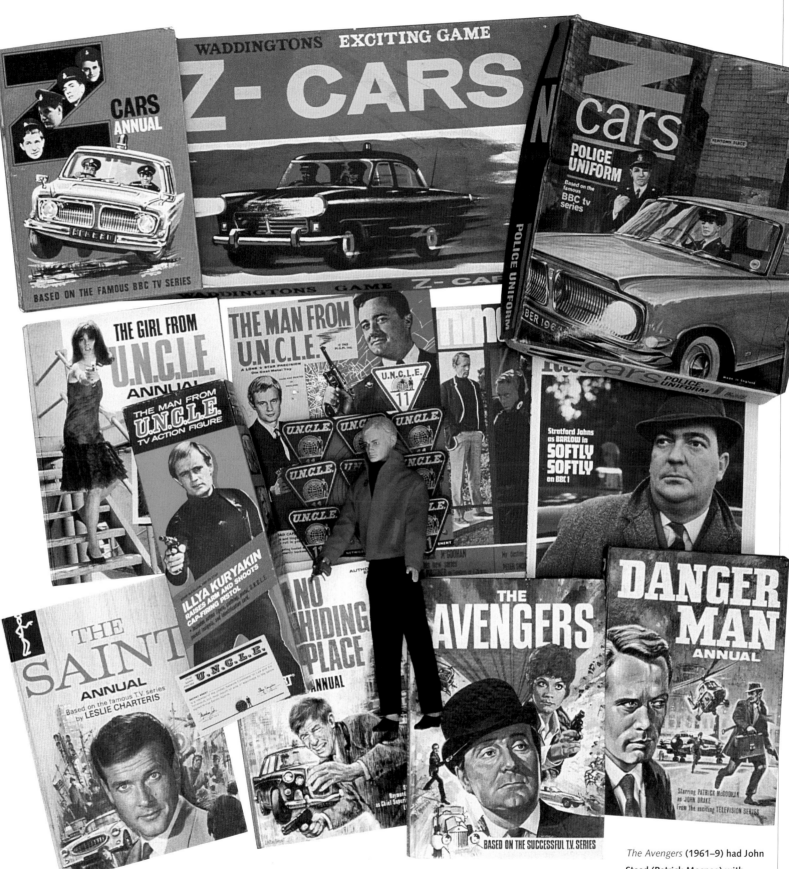

△ The police patrolmen of *Z Cars* drove their Ford Zephyrs on to the small screen in 1962 (until 1978). Their boss, Detective Inspector Charlie Barlow, was played by Stratford Johns, who went on to *Softly, Softly* (1966–76). *The Man from UNCLE* (1965–8) starred Robert Vaughn as Napoleon Solo and David McCallum as Ilya Kuryakin fighting the international criminals of THRUSH. *The Girl from UNCLE,* with Stephanie Powers, came in 1967. Roger Moore played Simon Templar, *The Saint* (1962–9), with his Volvo P1800. The classy spy series *The Avengers* (1961–9) had John Steed (Patrick Macnee) with accomplice Catherine Gale (Honor Blackman) and, from 1964, Emma Peel (Diana Rigg). *Danger Man* (1960–68) starred Patrick McGoohan, who became *The Prisoner* (1967–8).

Children's world

There was no shortage of children's entertainment on television. The two key production companies were the American cartoons of Hanna-Barbera and Britain's own puppeteer Gerry Anderson. Gordon Murray Puppets produced the distinctive animation of *Camberwick Green* in 1966 and then *Trumpton* in 1967, the latter famous for the fire brigade of Captain Flack and his men, Hugh, Pugh, Barney McGrew, Cuthbert, Dibble and Grubb. Frenchman Serge Danot created *The Magic Roundabout*, which aired in Britain from 1965 to 1977 and in which Florence looked after Ermintrude, Dougal, Zebedee, Dylan the rabbit and Brian the snail.

For older children *Dr Who* became compulsive viewing. The Daleks appeared in the second story, 'The Dead Planet' (1963), and the Cyberman in 1966. The first Dr Who was played by William Hartnell (1963–6), who was replaced by Patrick Troughton (1966–9).

▽ Hanna-Barbera cartoons included *Huckleberry Hound* (1960–64) from which came Yogi Bear and Mr Jinks the cat, the *Flintstones* (1961–6), and in 1963 *Deputy Dawg* and *The Jetsons*.

The comic *Tina* (1967) was enamoured of the mischievous Trolls. Ray Allen was the ventriloquist for Lord Charles. The foxy Basil Brush had his own show from 1968 to 1980.

△ Gerry Anderson's first television project with puppets had been *The Adventures of Twizzle* in 1956, but the director is best known for a string of successful futuristic stories – *Supercar* (1961), *Fireball XL5* (1963), *Stingray* (1964), with Troy Tempest, who worked for WASP, *Thunderbirds* (1965), *Captain Scarlet and the Mysterons* (1967) and *Joe 90* (1968). In 1965 the story comic *TV Century 21* came out to serialise the Gerry Anderson adventures and advertise merchandise like the Stingray scooter skate.

△ *Thunderbirds* featured the exploits of International Rescue. Jeff Tracy had five sons, each with his own vehicle – Scott, Virgil, Alan, Gordon and John were named after the first US astronauts in space. The other members of the team were the genius, Brains, and the London agent, Lady Penelope; her chauffeur, Parker, drove her pink Rolls-Royce, registration FAB 1.

Toys

With so many toys portraying TV characters, there was less scope in the 1960s for innovators lacking such links. Even so, a new wave of dolls arrived. Barbie, who had been developed in America by Mattell, made her début there in 1959; introduced as a teenage fashion model, she was far more curvaceous than previous dolls. Girls could now play with a doll who embodied and inspired their fantasies of teenage and adult life. The key feature of Barbie was the ever-expanding range of accessories and contemporary outfits, often created by leading designers. Barbie came to Britain in the early 1960s and was joined in 1963 by Sindy, made by Pedigree. 'Sindy is more than a doll, she's a real personality. The free, swinging, grown-up girl who dresses the way *she* likes.'

Action Man was another import from America, where he was launched under the name G.I. Joe by Hasbro in 1964. However, the backlash against the Vietnam war at the end of the 1960s led to the character being discontinued. Action Man came to Britain in 1966, manufactured under licence by Palitoy, who also produced a sailor and an aircraft pilot. For many years he was the favourite toy for boys. In 1968 he was given hands that could grip and in 1970 he acquired fibre hair. In 1984 the line was discontinued but he made a comeback in a new form in 1992.

◁ The Spacehopper bounced along in 1968 with its cartoon kangaroo face: 'Spacehopper is an exciting new idea in outdoor playthings, being great fun and good excitement for both children and adults.'

▽ Left to right: Barbie and boyfriend Ken (1961); Midge (1963), Barbie's best friend, 'a winsome young teenage doll'; Skipper (1964), Barbie's little sister; Ricky (1965), 'the cutest freckle-faced kid in town'; Allan (1964), Ken's buddy; Skooter (1965), a 'perky little pixie'; Francie joined in 1966 and the new craze for hair that grew (as in this example) followed in 1970.

▽ Launched in 1958 by Minimodels, Scalextric 'brings the excitement of motor racing right into your home where children and adults alike can enjoy the thrill of the race – the car travels at a scale speed of 130 mph on the straight'.

In Denmark in the 1930s Lego made wooden toys such as pull-along ducks on wheels. Plastic toys followed in 1947 and plastic bricks in 1955, but it was Lego's stud-and-tube coupling system of 1958 that made the firm successful.

▽ Sindy was created by Pedigree in 1963; her boyfriend Paul joined her in 1965 and Patch, her little sister, in 1966. Palitoy made Tressy from 1964 under licence. In 1965 she was joined by a little sister called Toots. Tammy's family from Ideal Toys arrived in 1962.

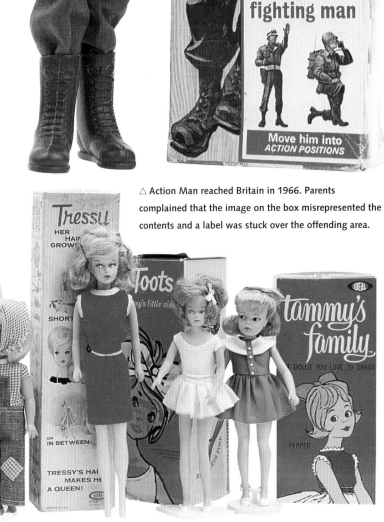

△ Action Man reached Britain in 1966. Parents complained that the image on the box misrepresented the contents and a label was stuck over the offending area.

Motoring

During the 1960s motoring in Britain took on a new outlook as the motorway system spread. It had begun in 1958 with the eight-mile Preston bypass and then the first section of the M1 in late 1959. Building for speed now led to the use on other main roads of double white lines to prohibit overtaking. But the big event was the invention in August 1959 of the Austin and Morris Mini cars. Designed by Alec Issigonis in response to the need for a small and fuel-efficient car, it was not an immediate success, even priced at just under £500. What saved it was its adoption by trendy Londoners who saw it as the answer to parking problems – Lord Snowdon, Peter Sellers and Twiggy all drove one – and when Paddy Hopkirk won the Monte Carlo Rally of 1964 in a Mini Cooper, sales rapidly accelerated. New cars of the 1960s included the Capri (1962), Consul Cortina (1963) and Ford Escort (1968), which replaced the Anglia.

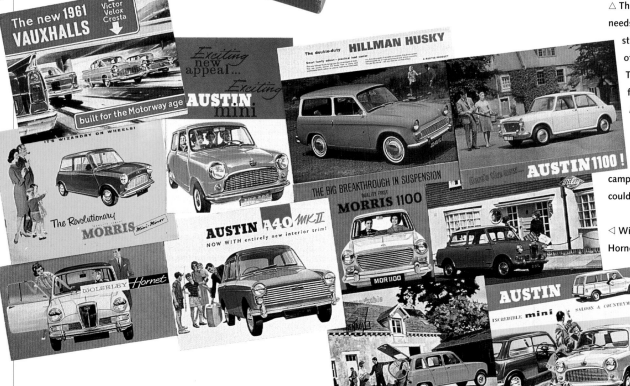

△ The E-type Jaguar encapsulated the needs of the male driver in 1961 – a streamlined body with the fastest speed of any production car: up to 150mph. The Dave Clark Five used the image for the cover of their album *Catch Us If You Can*, released in 1964. Petrol companies promised the thrill of speed and power: Esso's 'I've got a tiger in my tank' advertising campaign ran from 1963. The tiger's tail could be attached to an aerial or petrol cap.

◁ With fuel economy in mind, the Mini, Hornet and Riley Elf all made their mark. In 1962 the Austin 1100 and Morris 1100 were launched; hydrolastic fluid suspension gave a smooth ride. The Renault 4, with its innovative hatchback, arrived in 1961.

△ For schoolboys, getting behind the wheel could start early with an Airfix Junior Driver stuck to Dad's dashboard; or, for even greater realism, American chromed plastic controls (below)

including horn, gears, speedometer and windscreen wipers, all battery driven.

△ The British School of Motoring had been tutoring drivers since 1910, although there was no compulsory driving test until 1935. The Highway Code, introduced in 1931, had been continuously updated to take account of new regulations, such as the 'no parking' yellow lines (introduced gradually from 1956) and the 70mph speed limit from 1967. Diagrams for hand signals were dropped in 1975.

New frontiers

While American and Russian astronauts explored space and children saw their science-fiction toys become reality, many Britons discovered new frontiers thanks to package holidays on the Continent and beyond. Some airlines, for example Britannia Airways, founded in 1964, served mainly holiday makers, flying them to destinations like Spain, the Canary Islands, Malta, Bulgaria and North Africa. In 1960 BOAC inaugurated its first regular Boeing 707 service between London and New York. The BAC Super VC10 (below) came into service with BOAC in 1965 and was the first long-haul airliner to have its four engines sited on the rear of the fuselage, greatly reducing cabin noise. British European Airways (BEA) brought the Trident 1 aircraft into service during 1964, and the following year one of these airliners was the first to make an automatic landing on a commercial passenger service.

Many travellers brought back a taste for Continental cuisine and wanted to experiment in the kitchen with ingredients like pasta, aubergines, green peppers, herbs and garlic. Gradually a few shops began to respond to this demand and helpful books appeared, notably Elizabeth David's *French Provincial Cooking* (1960). In 1964 the first of Terence Conran's Habitat shops opened to provide the correct utensils.

△ Christopher Cockerell's great invention of the 1950s, the Hovercraft, began a passenger service in 1962 between Rhyl and Wallasey, and a cross-Channel service in 1968.

▽ Even though the world's largest passenger ship, Cunard's *Queen Elizabeth 2*, made her maiden voyage in 1969 to New York, the era of sea travel had ended and the jet age had begun.

MOON PROBE
AN EXCITING SPACE GAME

A Triang GAME

▷ Alongside realistic space toys there were still fictional flying saucers and imaginative space stations.

◁ In the late 1960s board games appeared like Waddington's Blast-Off! and Triang's Moon Probe, where players experiencing rocket engine failure and a drop of fuel pressure would have to 'go back three spaces and lose a turn'.

▽▷ The *Apollo X* rocket was launched in May 1969 with three astronauts for a rehearsal of the moon landing. Toys were either battery-powered, like *Apollo X*, or friction-driven, like the *Gemini* space capsule (around 1965).

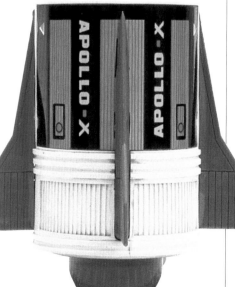

△ The three-stage rocket *Pioneer* was undergoing tests in 1960. In 1961 John Kennedy predicted, correctly, that the USA would put a man on the moon by the end of the decade.

▽ The ultimate in space vehicles was the *Apollo* Lunar Module. 'The Eagle has landed,' reported Armstrong as it touched down on the moon at Tranquillity Base. He returned with moon samples.

The 1970s

In 1971 Britain faced a mathematical challenge when decimalisation ousted shillings and pence. Two years later the country took a further leap and entered the Common Market. The Yes or No campaign to decide whether Britain should remain in the European Community produced an overwhelming Yes result, but it was not the end of 14 years of debate.

Fashion stayed on platform shoes and in flared trousers. Pop music ranged from glam-rock to punk while teenyboppers could choose between the clean-cut Osmonds or the tartan Bay City Rollers. Discomania reached its peak in 1977 when John Travolta strutted his stuff in *Saturday Night Fever*. Radio 1 and *Top of the Pops* began in the sixties, but now the DJs had been elevated to stardom – Tony Blackburn, David 'Diddy' Hamilton, Alan 'Fluff' Freeman, Dave Lee Travis, Noel Edmonds and Jimmy Saville, who moved to television with *Jim'll Fix It* in 1975. Noel Edmonds joined Keith Chegwin, John Craven and Maggie Philbin in *Multi Coloured Swap Shop* which was rivalled by *Tiswas* (1975), with Chris Tarrant, Lenny Henry and Sally James.

Comedy was king during the seventies: *Steptoe and Son* (1964–73) was still going strong, *Are You Being Served?* (1972–85), *Citizen Smith* (1977–80) with Robert Lindsay, *Some Mothers Do 'Ave 'Em* (1973–8) with Michael Crawford. But British comedy was never the same after *Monty Python's Flying Circus* (1969–74) with Michael Palin, Terry Jones, Eric Idle, Graham Chapman and John Cleese (who moved on to *Fawlty Towers* in 1975). Colour television did more than add colour to the balls in televised snooker, it brought home the realism of war. TV news reports showing the carnage and horror of Vietnam shocked many people into speaking out against the war.

Many shops now had mail order catalogues, for example Habitat and Mothercare (shown above left). It was also a time of high inflation – a Mars bar cost three times as much by the end of the decade.

The era of global travel began in 1970 when the first Pan Am Boeing 747 jet landed at Heathrow. Popular on the roads were the Aston Martin, Triumph TR7, two door Capri and MGB GT (1978). The novelty vehicle was the Reliant Bond Bug (1970), which didn't last quite as long as eight track tapes (see p. 5).

Events

It was a decade of strikes, postal workers, miners and dustmen, culminating with the 'winter of discontent' in 1979 when ITV went off the air for five months. A three-day week was imposed during February 1972 to save on electricity. The Arab-Israeli war of October 1973 caused a worldwide oil shortage and as petrol prices soared so did inflation, to 26 per cent by 1975.

During the summer of 1976 the weather turned so dry that water supplies reached critically low levels. The government appointed their minister for sport, Dennis Howell, to oversee the Drought Act and the implementation of water restrictions.

◁ *Private Eye* caught the essential news: President Nixon resigned over the Watergate scandal in 1974, with streaking and panda mating in the same year; Harold Wilson looked for 'signs of recovery' in 1976.

△ After years of planning and with a public fearful of the outcome, the changeover to decimal currency happened on 15 February 1971. Decimal conversion charts could not be avoided – chocolate coins at least gave sweet relief.

◁ The Queen's Silver Jubilee of 1977 reached onto the supermarket shelves as Jubilade soft drink, ice cream, ice lollies, mousse and margarine. Festive hats were an optional extra, as were 'stuff the jubilee' badges.

▷ After years of trials, Concorde came into service in 1976 with British Airways, giving a boost to the sales of toy models.

British airways

G-BBDG

Laker
SUMMER 1978 HOLIDAYS

PRICE GUARANTEE See page 2

Clarksons CRUISES

1973
8,11,12, and 15 day cruises
Flights from Manchester, Bristol, Luton or Gatwick
East & West Mediterranean, Canaries, Russia & the Danube

Ink

GAY!

Demand the right

GAY NEWS

N°5 10p

LOOK NOW

COSMOPOLITAN

◁ Cosmopolitan magazine arrived in Britain in 1972: 'Jilly Cooper tells what makes these men fantastic lovers'; the gay community came out in the early 1970s and the image of revolutionary Che Guevara (executed in Bolivia in 1967) became the radical icon.

△ Freddie Laker set up his cut-price tours business in 1966 and Skytrain undercut the big airlines from 1977 but it collapsed in 1982. Clarksons also collapsed, leaving hundreds of holiday makers stranded in 1974.

▽ Buzby presided over the Trimphone which came in 1975 to give 'style to your home'. By 1977 the Trimphone had joined 'the press-button age'.

INTERSTATE
THE MOST EXCITING VIDEO GAME FOR THE MODERN FAMILY

INTERSTATE
THE MOST EXCITING VIDEO GAME FOR THE MODERN FAMILY
WORKS ON MOST COLOR OR BLACK AND WHITE TV

◁ Interactive television games such as Interstate started a revolutionary craze in the late 1970s.

BUZBY

A TRIMPHONE GIVES STYLE TO YOUR HOME

SERVE   RESET

Fashion

The influence of pop music on fashion continued with glam-rock and then punk. For both men and women, platform shoes were the new rage as were flared trousers, especially flared denim jeans – some flared from the knee and were known as loons. In the early 1970s hot pants for women were a novelty and the other extreme, maxi skirts and maxi coats, could give a seductive flash of leg.

Punks were out to shock. Hair was cropped short but then extended in outlandish sculptures, such as a Mohican style dyed bright pink. Skinhead culture emerged at the end of this decade, with its menacing combination of crew cut and bovver boot.

Slowly the discreet clothes label inside a garment moved to the outside, where the designer label made a style statement – that the wearer could afford the streetwise gear.

▽ **Home accessories included the fibre optic and lava lamps, the executive toy Newton's balls, Andy Warhol's rendition of Marilyn Monroe and Roy** Lichtenstein-style pop graphics. The reflection in the mirror is of Peter Blake's pop picture Babe Rainbow (1968).

△ Beachwear for the Kodak girls evolved into a fashion parade. The Instamatic had been the snap-happy camera since 1968.

△▽ Platform shoes and flares became the unisex fashion statement. Girls' dolls like Sindy were dressed in the latest fashions with accessories to match. Tressy's hair could be combed and teased into any number of styles, from 'Mod' bob to side plait. In 1973 Mary Quant decided to create a range of outfits for her own Daisy dolls, to be 'the best-dressed doll in the world'.

Products

The need to find new products, new flavours and new tastes never diminishes. Cigarette manufacturers tried out a tobacco substitute in 1977 (see opposite), sometimes referred to as NSM (new smoking material); it did not contain nicotine, but nor did it 'taste' right for smokers, so the brands were withdrawn. In 1975 another type of substitute was Soya Choice Mince made from textured soya protein.

Characters continued to add value to brands. Fred the Homepride flour grader had been so successful in TV commercials that from 1969 a series of kitchen accessories were created. Yogurt and other children's foods were adorned with the 'behaviour type' Mr Men people created by Roger Hargreaves and published since 1971.

◁ Arriving around 1970, the Party Four or Party Seven were a must for any serious revelling – the difficulty arose when opening the huge can as the contents could cause an surprise shower if not allowed to settle first.

△ Biba moved into a major department store in the early 1970s to sell much more than clothes and cosmetics. Its food store sold everything from Biba baked beans to soap flakes, all co-ordinated with the retro Biba graphics.

▽ Toiletries for men blossomed. Brut found new impetus from television commercials that showed Henry Cooper splashing it all over; Barry Sheen and Kevin Keegan were in support. Soap-on-a-rope, such as 'Enry's 'Ammer, was a popular novelty item.

△ New ready-made foods such as pizza were on the increase (Pizza Hut had begun in 1965). Golden Nuggets were in the shops from 1970–79 (relaunched in 1999). The Aztec bar hung around from 1968–77. At the end of the 1970s Monster Munch snacks were launched together with the instant foods of Golden Wonder's Pot Noodle and Batchelor's snackpot.

▷ Character toiletries featured strongly. Ken Dodd and his Diddymen (1969–72) were based in Diddyland, where Knotty Ash was famous for its jam butty mines.

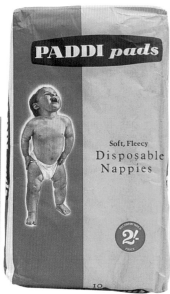

△ Nappies went through a transformation. Paddi Pads had arrived in the late 1960s, Snugglers in 1975 (becoming brand leaders with their all-in-one nappy and plastic pants) and Pampers in 1982.

▽ In the early 1970s Aqua Manda targeted teens and girls in their twenties; with its fragrance of flower power, it 'makes your body more beautiful'.

Television

With the success of the Manchester-based *Coronation Street*, a rival 'soap' had started in 1964 in the Central TV region. Based in the Midlands, the Crossroads Motel opened its doors to a barrage of criticism for its poor production, and yet this endeared it to its fans. Screened nationally from 1972–88 it reached a peak of popularity in 1978 with over 17 million viewers. *Emmerdale Farm,* set in the Yorkshire Dales, started in 1979.

For children there was *Catweazle* (1970), *Rainbow* (1972), and *Bagpuss* (1974), and for adults there were series such as *On the Buses* (1970–75), *Kojak* (1974–8) and *The New Avengers* (1976).

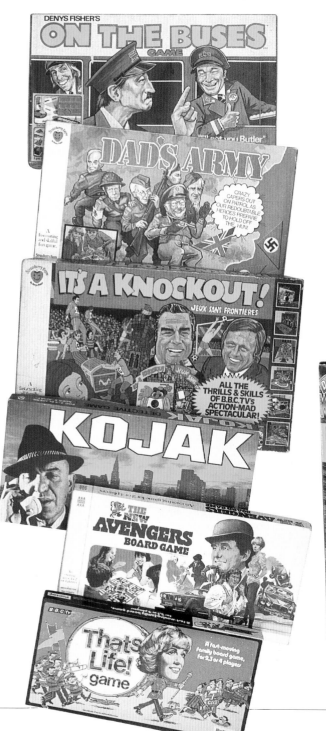

△ First shown in Britain 1969–70, *Star Trek* took time to become a cult phenomenon. Aboard the USS *Enterprise* were Captain Kirk, the Vulcan Mr Spock and chief engineer Montgomery Scott.

▽ By the 1970s Dr Who was played by John Pertwee (1969–74) and Tom Baker (1974–81). Along with Daleks, children had the Tardis time machine and K-9.

▽ The inspiration of Jim Henson, *The Muppet Show* began on ITV in 1976 with Kermit the Frog, Miss Piggy, Fozzie Bear, The Great Gonzo, Animal, Scooter and the two hecklers Waldorf and Statler.

△ From the USA came Henry Winkler as The Fonz in *Happy Days* (1975–84), *Starsky and Hutch* (1976–81) with Paul Michael Glaser and David Soul and *Charlie's Angels* (1977–82). British drama focused on *Upstairs Downstairs* (1971–5) and comedy on *The Good LIfe* (1974–8) and *Fawlty Towers* (1975 and 1979).

▽ *Play School* had begun in 1964 and lasted until 1988 with the help of toys like Humpty (below), Big and Little Ted and Jemima.

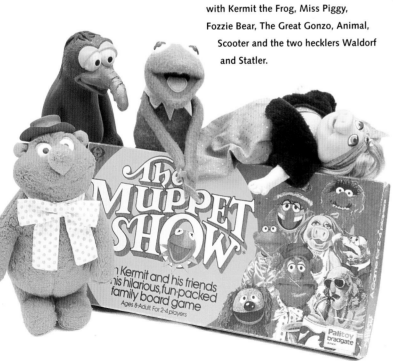

Music

As the pop music scene matured so its audience widened to a younger age group – the teeny boppers. David Cassidy appeared in *The Partridge Family* (1970–74) and had a number of hits, such as *How Can I Be Sure* (1972). The Jackson 5 brothers' popularity grew, especially when the youngest, Michael, had a solo hit with *Off The Wall* (1979). The Osmonds, six brothers who stormed the UK in 1972, had hits such as *Puppy Love*. The youngest, Jimmy, had a solo number one with *Long Haired Lover From Liverpool* (1976). The Osmonds' sister, Marie, had a hit with *Paper Roses* (1973). Britain's own idol was David Essex who played Jesus in the rock musical *Godspell* and starred in the film *That'll Be The Day* (1973).

◁ To choose a name, a pin was stuck in a map of America. The Bay City Rollers from Edinburgh were born. The height of Rollermania, with its tartan outfits and other souvenirs, came in 1974 with number one hits *Bye Bye Baby* and *Give a Little Love*.

△ Music festivals became part of the pop scene. Woodstock in 1969 was a pivotal event in America, featuring many of the musical greats, while in Britain the first Isle of Wight Festival was staged in 1969, the second in 1970.

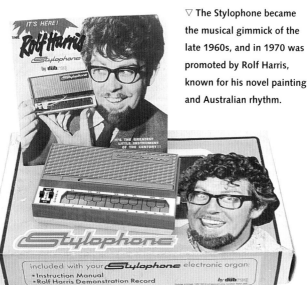

▽ The Stylophone became the musical gimmick of the late 1960s, and in 1970 was promoted by Rolf Harris, known for his novel painting and Australian rhythm.

△ Mark Bolan (with tartan trousers) headed the glam rock movement with T. Rex and *Electric Warrior* (1971). Then came David Bowie with *Ziggy Stardust* (1972). Big names included Elton John, Led Zeppelin, Kiss, Genesis, Pink Floyd and Queen. ABBA won Eurovision 1974 with *Waterloo*; then came *S.O.S.* and *Mamma Mia* (1975).

▽ The Sex Pistols were formed in 1975, originally to publicise Vivienne Westwood's clothes. Many of their gigs, led by Jonny Rotten, became the focal point for a disillusioned youth.

Toys

The success of vinyl plastics developed during the 1950s had enabled dolls such as Barbie, Sindy and Action Man to be made cheaply and yet with realistic features. Along with other dolls such as the Six Million Dollar Man, they became favourite gifts for children. The power of the TV commercial prior to Christmas put pressure on parents' purses.

Peer pressure also fed the need to have the latest bike, the Chopper, or the skateboard with the go-fast graphics to give any child the necessary street cred. During 1977 over one million skateboards were sold in the UK – but no one knows the sales for Roger de Courcey's boggle-eyed Nookie Bear (opposite).

◁ The annoying sound of 1971 was that of people trying to master the art of Klackers. They caused numerous injuries and were banned in some schools.

▽ In the *Six Million Dollar Man* (1974–8), astronaut Steve Austin (Lee Majors) had his body rebuilt after a crash landing, with atomic electronic devices to give him superhuman powers. *The Bionic Woman* was played by Lindsay Wagner, and *Wonder Woman* (1978–80) starred Lynda Carter.

△ Raleigh's Chopper came out in 1970, originally priced at £32. The concept was initiated by Tom Karen, who also worked on the Bond Bug (see p.172). The Chipper (with detachable cross bar) arrived in 1971 for girls, and the Tomahawk for younger boys came in 1972.

◁ Bored by the lack of waves, some American surfers devised a way of 'surfing' on land in the mid-sixties – the skateboard; but it was not until 1973 that wheels of the plastic compound urethane enabled skateboarding to take off.

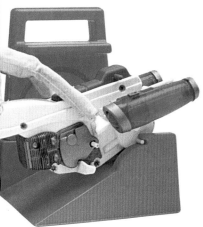

◁ Evel Knievel was the American daredevil motor bike stunt rider who could jump 52 cars. The toys were a hit around 1972–3, especially in the US.

◁ *Crossfire* was heavily promoted in 1971 on television, but never lived up to expectations.

▷ The beginner's outfit with which to follow in the master's footsteps – 'all the elements of real golf' included in a three-foot box.

▽ In 1958 Michael Bond's book *A Bear Called Paddington* was published. In 1972 the toy Paddington Bear became popular with the addition of wellington boots to help him stand.

Film

While cinema-going in the 1960s had declined, there were many reasons during the seventies for returning to the movies. A surprisingly popular film was *MASH* (1970) set in the Korean War – a film that drew parallels with the Vietnam War that was in full swing at the time. A TV series followed (1973–84), remembered for a host of characters such as 'Hot Lips' Houlihan. In 1971 Clint Eastwood found a new hero with *Dirty Harry*, followed by *Magnum Force* (1974). *The French Connection* (1971) with Gene Hackman, *The Godfather* (1971) with Marlon Brando – also starring in *Last Tango in Paris* (1972) – and *Cabaret* (1972) with Liza Minelli were all memorable in different ways. Steven Spielberg's *Jaws* (1975) with its gripping music was the money-spinner of its day. Jack Nicholson in *One Flew Over the Cuckoo's Nest* (1975) won critical acclaim, as did *All The President's Men* (1976).

△ Roger Moore became James Bond in *Live and Let Die* (1973), the first of his seven Bond movies, which included *Moonraker* (1979) and its space shuttle.

May the force be with you

1970s

▷ John Travolta cruised in with *Saturday Night Fever* (1977) – the soundtrack sold over 30 million copies. Travolta followed up with *Grease* (1978). *The Sting* (1973) was famous for its theme tune.

◁ *Star Wars* (1977) won seven Academy Awards, including one for visual effects. The main participants were Luke Skywalker, Han Solo, Princess Leia, the Jedi warrior Obi-Wan Kenobi and Darth Vader, the black-clad tyrant of the Empire. The two androids C3PO and R2D2 injected some comic relief. Two sequels followed: *The Empire Strikes Back* (1980) and *Return of the Jedi* (1983). In 1999 the blockbuster 'prequel' *The Phantom Menace* was released.

▷ Some of Peter Sellers's zaniest acting came in the role of the incompetent Inspector Clouseau: *The Pink Panther* (1963), *A Shot in the Dark* (1964) and *The Return of the Pink Panther* (1974).

The 1980s

True romance may not have worked for Charles and Di or for Andrew and Fergie, but their weddings were two of the highlights of the 1980s, watched by over 700 million people worldwide. The world was by now a global village, but a village that became increasingly vulnerable to the threat of a new disease first identified in 1981 – the AIDS virus.

The silicone micro-chip was now served with everything to further the technological revolution, providing pocket calculators, word processors like the Sinclair ZX home computer of the early 1980s and Amstrad PCW 9512 of 1987 (shown below), home video recorders and more advanced electronic games. Fibreoptics began to replace telephone cables, and compact discs, camcorders, cordless phones and rather bulky mobile phones all began to appear.

There was a growing concern over ecological and environmental issues such as acid rain, chemical emissions and the effect of CFCs on the ozone layer. More bottle banks opened. There was also concern over the ingredients and additives in processed foods. In the kitchen, the microwave oven (first patented in the USA in 1945) benefitted those with a busy lifestyle – such as Yuppies (young urban professionals). Bar codes on packaging, Space Dust (see p.5) and the squeezable plastic ketchup bottle were all innovations.

Brookside (1982) and *Eastenders* (1985) were the new British soaps, while other popular shows included *Terry and June*, *'Allo 'Allo*, *Blackadder*, *Hi-De-Hi*, *Only Fools and Horses* and *The Hitchhikers' Guide to the Galaxy* (1981).

Politically, the eighties were dominated by the Conservative government of Margaret Thatcher, who took on the trade unions and privatised many state-owned industries. These were turbulent times. Britons were involved in unrest abroad in the Falklands War and the Middle East hostage crisis. At home there was a string of disasters: the Bradford stadium fire (1985), the wreck of the *Herald of Free Enterprise* at Zeebrugge (1987), the King's Cross inferno (1987), the Pan Am crash at Lockerbie (1988), and the Hillsborough football crush (1989). On the world stage the Russian leader Mikhail Gorbachev added two words to the Western vocabulary – perestroika and glasnost – and the iron curtain was swept away.

Events

In 1980 the big questions were who shot J.R. in the soap *Dallas*, who was Prince Charles going to marry, and how much longer would you devote to solving the Rubik's Cube puzzle? Beyond these frivolous questions lay more dramatic events. In 1982 Argentina invaded the Falkland Islands and Britain went to war. HMS *Sheffield* was destroyed by Exocet missiles, to the disbelief of the Admiralty. Two days earlier the Argentine cruiser *Belgrano* had been sunk by torpedoes. Within twelve weeks the Falklands had been recaptured.

Cracks appeared in the Communist world when in November 1989 the Berlin Wall, which had stood for 40 years, was demolished, and in Romania the Communist dictator Nicolae Ceausescu was overthrown and executed in December of that year.

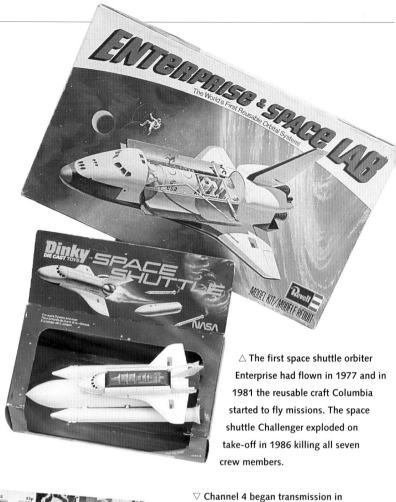

△ The first space shuttle orbiter Enterprise had flown in 1977 and in 1981 the reusable craft Columbia started to fly missions. The space shuttle Challenger exploded on take-off in 1986 killing all seven crew members.

◁ Latex mimics of famous people, especially politicians, formed the innovative *Spitting Image* TV satire that lasted from 1984 through two general elections to 1996.

▽ Channel 4 began transmission in November 1982. TV-am began in February 1983, but failed to gain sufficient audiences. The original presenters were replaced by Anne Diamond and Nick Owen later that year. To further aid the survival of TV-am, the 'superstar' Roland Rat and his friend Kevin also came aboard in 1983.

▽ Prince Andrew married Sarah Ferguson in Westminster Abbey on 23 July 1986. They had two daughters, Beatrice and Eugenie, but separated in 1992.

△ On 30 July 1981 at St Paul's Cathedral, the Prince of Wales married Lady Diana Spencer. They had been engaged since February. Diana's wedding dress was created by David and Elizabeth Emanuel and the royal occasion was watched by a worldwide TV audience of some 700 million. Amongst the traditional souvenirs were some novelties – one mug had a handle formed by one of Charles's ears, there were 'rock' T-shirts and cut-out paper dolls, a Rubik's Cube and a pair of waving hands that could be fixed to car windows to look as if Charles and Di were in the back seat. The Princess of Wales gave birth to their first child, William, in 1982, and their second son, Henry, followed in 1984.

Film and television

American soaps, with their lavish sets and costumes, dominated British television. *Dallas* had begun in 1978 (until 1991) with J. R. Ewing (Larry Hagman), his brother Bobby (Patrick Duffy) and J. R.'s wife Sue Ellen (Linda Gray). By 1980 it was the most popular TV series in the world, climaxing in the cliffhanger episode leaving everyone wondering who shot J.R. Its rival was *Dynasty* (1982–9), with Denver millionaire Blake Carrington (John Forsythe) and his scheming ex-wife Alexis (Joan Collins). Other US imports included *Mork and Mindy* (1979–83), which launched the career of Robin Williams, *The Dukes of Hazard* (1979–85), *Taxi* (1980–85), *Cagney and Lacey* (1982–8), *Knight Rider* (1983–7), *The A Team* (1984–8) with Mr T (see p. 197) and, still going strong from the seventies, *Sesame Street*.

△ *Eastenders* went on the air in 1985. The twice-weekly soap from Albert Square featured the Beales, the Fowlers and Den and Angie at the Queen Vic.

△ ▷ Gordon the Gopher was the loveable squeaky puppet that assisted Philip Schofield on BBC's Saturday morning show *Live and Kicking*. Edd the Duck was another assistant at the end of the 1980s, while the Crow stood by on *Saturday Super Store*. Alternative comedy on TV began with *The Young Ones* in 1982, and carried on with *French and Saunders* in 1987. *Hi-De-Hi!* (1980–89), *Yes, Minister* (1980–86), *'Allo, 'Allo* (1982–92) and *Blackadder* (1983–9) all became comedy classics.

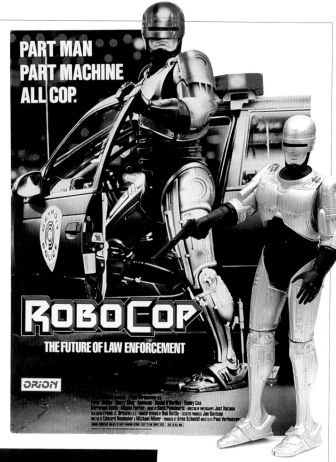

△ Both Buck Rogers and Flash Gordon first came to Britain in the late thirties as cartoon strips. Now they reappeared in films – *Buck Rogers* in 1979 and *Flash Gordon* in 1980.

▷ The part of *RoboCop* (1987), part man and part machine, was played by Peter Weller and followed the successful concept of the *Six Million Dollar Man* – a human form with bionic powers.

◁ Steven Spielberg's *ET: The Extra-Terrestrial* (1982) was the box office success of the decade, making the wrinkled 'phone home' creature into a natural merchandizing icon. *The Black Hole*, which reached the UK in 1980, also had plenty of merchandizing. A busy Harrison Ford starred in blockbusters *Raiders of the Lost Ark* (1981), *Bladerunner* (1982), and the *Star Wars* sequels the *Empire Strikes Back* (1980) and *Return of the Jedi* (1983). Other hits included *Tootsie* (1982) with Dustin Hoffman, *Ghostbusters* (1984), *Back to the Future* (1985) with Michael J. Fox, *Top Gun* (1986) with Tom Cruise, *Fatal Attraction* (1987) with Michael Douglas and Glenn Close and *Batman* (1989). British films included *Chariots of Fire* (1981), *A Room With a View* (1985) and *Gandhi* (1982).

1980s

Pop music

The power of pop made itself heard in 1984 when Boomtown Rats singer Bob Geldof and Midge Ure of Ultravox organized help for starving people in Ethiopia. Britain's top rock stars joined together to form Band Aid, producing a single *Do They Know It's Christmas?* The following year Geldof organized Live Aid – two huge concerts held simultaneously at London's Wembley Stadium and JFK Stadium in Philadelphia. Watched by 1.5 billion people on television, over £50 million was raised to help famine relief in Africa. The pop cast included Status Quo, Sting, Queen, David Bowie, Paul McCartney, Joan Baez, Madonna, Eric Clapton, Mick Jagger, Led Zeppelin, Duran Duran and Bob Dylan. Phil Collins crossed the Atlantic on Concorde to perform at both shows.

▽ Along with novelty picture discs (from the late 1970s), came compact discs (CDs) in 1983. From America the funky sounds of Prince culminated with the album *Purple Rain* (1984), and at the same time the material girl Madonna popped to fame in the UK with *Holiday* and the hit album *Like A Virgin*. Headbangers thrived on the heavy metal anthems of groups such as Iron Maiden, while more danceable tunes came from Wham!, with the chart topping *Wake Me Up Before You Go Go* (1984). Sting went solo after the Police split in 1986, and Dublin's U2 were one of the most successful bands of the eighties. The all-girl trio Bananarama did it right with *It Ain't What You Do It's The Way That You Do It* in 1982.

△▷ Inspired by Live Aid, Comic Relief started plastering red noses everywhere in 1986, and in 1980 the BBC's Children in Need began, adopting Pudsey Bear as its symbol in 1986.

◁ With the popularity of jogging came the Sony Walkman (the first version in 1979 and Walkman II in 1981), and headphone radios like Chegger's Jogger, which bore the face of Keith Chegwin, presenter of BBC's *Cheggers Plays Pop*. The first Next mail-order catalogue (1988) shows accessories made of fashionable black plastic.

▷ The cool dude of the eighties would make his presence felt by lugging around on his shoulder the ghetto blaster radio, blaring out music to everyone's annoyance.

△ In 1982 Michael Jackson's *Thriller* was a phenomenon that sold 48 million albums worldwide, although in Britain this was outsold by his next album *Bad* (1987). The New Romantics carried on the legacy of Glam Rock. Many artists used heavy make-up, including Adam and the Ants (*Kings of the Wild Frontier*, 1980), Culture Club (*Do You Really Want To Hurt Me?*, 1982, and *Karma Chameleon*, 1983) and Toyah (*Four From Toyah*, 1981).

Toys

Even with television- and film-generated merchandising, there was still a huge market that continued to buy more traditional toys such as jigsaw puzzles, dolls, teddy bears and many other soft toys. Nursery and activity toys for toddlers were almost exclusively ·made from the all-conquering plastic. Perennial games such as Monopoly, Scrabble and Cluedo were still favourites, to be joined by Trivial Pursuit, the new quiz game from Canada that was aimed at adults. Toy cars, trains and motor race tracks like Scalextric remained popular. The spacehopper (see p. 166) had extended into Happy Hoppers and Mr Bounce Hopper, while stunt kites had been becoming increasingly elaborate since the 1970s. Even Subbuteo had not been badly affected by the new electronic games.

Advances in computer technology enabled games programmes to be played on hand-held consoles such as Atari's Space Invaders and Nintendo's Game Boy, introduced in 1983.

▷ Cabbage Patch Kids from Mattel went on sale in the US in 1983 and as Christmas approached, parents became increasingly desperate to 'adopt' one for their child. 75 millions were sold worldwide in 12 years.

△ The Nike Air Max, the first air shoe with a technical sole came out in 1987, while Dr Martens boots had been around since 1945. Adidas and Reebok were other high-profile brands.

△ The BMX Burner from Raleigh was the action bike of 1982; it was capable of stunt tricks and riders were encouraged to wear protective clothes and head gear. Also popular were the mountain bikes developed in California during the 1970s.

△ The springboard for so many toys was television or film or occasionally a book, such as Raymond Briggs's *The Snowman* (1979). Other soft toys were produced for the cat Garfield, Keith Harris's duck Orville (*Orville's Song* reached number four in Christmas 1982) and the Gremlins, whose film appeared in 1984. Bendy Toys had been popular since the 1950s, and still produced a range of children's favourites such as Postman Pat and Tony Hart's Morph. Dusty Bin was a character from the ITV show *3–2–1*.

◁ Transforming robots were a craze from 1984, led by Hasbro, The film *Transformers* came out in 1986, the date of the model shown here of the baddie Galvatron, leader of the Decepticons.

The 1990s

Millions pinned their hopes on the luck of the draw when the National Lottery started in 1994, and even watching *Who Wants to be a Millionaire* had its attractions. Children's crazes ranged from Tamagotchi (virtual pets) to dinosaurs

and yo-yos (yet again). There was animated entertainment to suite every taste – kids loved *Teenage Mutant Hero Turtles*, *The Lion King* and *Toy Story*; everyone enjoyed *Wallace & Gromit*; and *The Simpsons* and *South Park* earned a cult following with grownups.

Britain had a wave of cinema successes with *Four Weddings and a Funeral*, *The Full Monty* and *Shakespeare in Love*. But the big blockbusters still came from Hollywood: *Jurassic Park*, *Titanic*, and *The Phantom Menace*. Many ordinary people were made famous by real-life docudramas, including *Airport*, *Pet Rescue* and *The Cruise*. The most sensational of these was without doubt the trial-by-television of American football star O. J. Simpson.

Britain drew closer to Europe when the Channel Tunnel rail service began in 1995. New Labour ended 18 years of Conservative rule in 1997, and Hong Kong, a British colony since 1842, was returned to China.

War was again in the headlines when Iraq invaded Kuwait in 1990 and the atrocities in Yugoslavia appeared to know no bounds. But the possibility of peace in the Middle East and Northern Ireland came closer. Tragic deaths shocked the

nation: in 1996 schoolchildren and teachers were gunned down in Dunblane, Scotland, and in 1999 the television presenter Jill Dando was shot outside her home. The biggest shock of all, however, was undoubtedly the news that Princess Diana had been killed in a car accident on 1 September 1997.

By the end of the 20th century a mass market service economy for all had replaced the use of servants by the few; the advances of the information superhighway and the world wide web seemed to offer unlimited human advancement – and yet *Men Behaving Badly* was a popular new sitcom. Debate focussed on cloning, genetically modified food and Internet censorship. In the 21st century we will no doubt complain about the cost of a holiday in space.

Licensed characters

One of the earliest comic characters was Ally Sloper (see p.17) who appeared in *Judy* magazine from 1867, and got his own publication, *Ally Sloper's Half Holiday*, in 1884. He was used on toys and promotional cards in the 1890s and during the 1920s and 1930s Benteshaw & Turner of Manchester produced Ally Sloper's Favourite Relish, 'Directions: take plenty of it with everything'. The licensing of characters reached new dimensions with the success of Mickey Mouse and other Disney animations during the 1930s (see p.94). Disney creations continue to pour out and yet Mickey Mouse has become the perennial survivor. Licensing has developed into a huge industry interlinked with film and television. During the 1990s many children's favourites made a comeback, including Noddy and Thomas the Tank Engine.

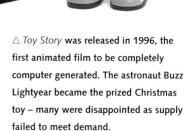

△ *Toy Story* was released in 1996, the first animated film to be completely computer generated. The astronaut Buzz Lightyear became the prized Christmas toy – many were disappointed as supply failed to meet demand.

◁ During 1990 and 1991 the Teenage Mutant Hero Turtles – Michaelangelo, Donatello, Raphael and Leonardo – were on film and television, and the shops were full of Turtle merchandise. The crime-fighting Turtle warriors practised the ancient Japanese art of Ninjitsu and loved to eat pizza – a natural link for pizza promotion. 'Cowabunga!'

▽ Around since the 1970s, shaped bubble bath containers burst forth in the 1990s. They included Nick Park's Wallace & Gromit (1990), Mr Blobby from *Noel's House Party* (1992) and Bart Simpson, the kid with attitude, who appeared on Sky from 1990.

△ Computer games advanced; the new star of 1991 was Sega's Sonic the Hedgehog, overtaking Nintendo's Super Mario Brothers.

▷ The Teletubbies were the creation of Anne Wood and the company Ragdoll, and appeared on BBC2 early in 1997. By August it was reported in Stratford-upon-Avon that there were more visitors asking where the Teletubbies lived than where Shakespeare's birthplace was. Left to right: Po, Tinky Winky, Laa-Laa and Dipsey.

△ The film *Titanic* (1997) was an enormous hit and yet failed to capitalize on merchandizing potential, unlike *Jurassic Park* (1993). *The Lion King* (1994), *Independence Day* (1996), *Mars Attacks!* (1997), *Aladdin* (1992) and *GoldenEye* (1996) with Pierce Brosnan as the new Bond. Other major movies included Tom Hanks in *Forrest Gump* (1994), Spielberg's *Schindler's List* (1994) and Anthony Hopkins in *Silence of the Lambs* (1991).

Music and fashion

For a time in the early 1990s MC Hammer made his mark on the rap scene, and there was music for the teeny boppers from Bros and Right Said Fred (see below). George Michael had left Wham! in 1986 to start a successful solo career, while Robbie Williams split from Take That in 1996 and by the following year had established his star rating with the album *Life Thru a Lens*. Britpop hit the scene in 1994 with groups like Suede (*Stay Together*), Blur (*Parklife*), Pulp (*Different Class*) and Oasis, fronted by brothers Liam and Noel Gallagher with a reputation for trouble, reaching the top with their first album *Definitely Maybe*. But undoubtedly the phenomenon of the decade was the sudden arrival of Girl Power that swept over everything in a tidal wave, the ultimate consumer hype that affected ideas and fashion, and put girls on a new platform.

△ The ever-growing interest in fashion made the top models into icons – and some were made into dolls like Germany's Claudia Schiffer and Britain's Naomi Campbell. Barbie kept up, with her fashion outfit for working out while listening to music, which Sindy also did whilst rollerblading.

△ The mid-nineties saw the arrival of a new drinks market – alcopops. These fancy alcoholic sweet drinks had funky names and colourful designs.

▷ Boyzone had been pulled together by a Dublin club owner in 1993 and hit the charts with *Love Me For A Reason* in 1995. Take That's success happened with chart-topper *Pray* (1993) a year after being formed. The group split in 1995–6 with Gary Barlow and Robbie Williams moving on to more success.

△ Girl Power hit Britain in 1996. The Spice Girls were formed in 1993, their alter egos created by *Top of the Pops* magazine: Geri Halliwell (Ginger Spice), Melanie Chisholm (Sporty Spice), Melanie Brown (Scary Spice), Emma Bunton (Baby Spice) and Victoria Adams (Posh Spice). They had three number one hits in 1996 with *Wannabe*, *Say You'll Be There* and *2 Become 1*. The movie *Spiceworld* came out in 1998 just before Geri left suddenly in May – and then there were four.

Index

Author's acknowledgments

The 500,000 items in the Robert Opie Collection have been raided to produce the images in this book. Even by cramming in some 2,500 memorable moments it has clearly been impossible to include everyone's favourite memory, but hopefully there will be plenty for all here, and many more may be sparked off by a visit to the Museum of Brands, Packaging and Advertising in London's Notting Hill (0207 908 0880) where much of the content of this book is on display.

My thanks to the hundreds of authors who have themselves gone through the tortures of assembling a book, thus sharing their knowledge; to those dealers and fellow collectors whose enthusiasm has helped me over 30 years of collecting and researching; to Jan and Edward Garling for their tremendous support in Gloucester; and to my parents for being the right sort of parents.

Thank you also to all those involved in the production of this book, especially to Elisabeth Faber, Dan Newman and Richard Dawes; to Penelope Cream and Jane Royston; and to my trusty Pentax camera.